26 Letters

26 Letters
Illuminating the Alphabet

Edited by Freda Sack, John Simmons and Tim Rich

CYAN

"A love of letters is the beginning of typographical wisdom. That is, the love of letters as literature and the love of letters as physical entities, having abstract beauty of their own, apart from the ideas they may express."

John R. Biggs, typographer and writer

Celebrating the exhibition held at the British Library in autumn 2004 as part of the London Design Festival

First published in Great Britain in 2004 by

Cyan Communications Limited
4.3 The Ziggurat
60–66 Saffron Hill
London EC1N 8QX
www.cyanbooks.com

A CIP record for this book is available from the British Library

ISBN 1-904879-15-2

Book design by Peter Dawson at Grade Design Consultants, London

Foundry Monoline typeface kindly supplied by The Foundry, London
Text set in Foundry Monoline Light

Printed in Great Britain by Good News Press
Bound by Hunter and Foulis
Printed on Zanders Mega Matt 150gsm (text) and Vanguard Lime Green 230mic (endpapers)
Paper supplied by Mason's Paper Company

Contents

Introduction

Freda Sack + John Simmons

Writing and typographic design: twin disciplines that sometimes fail to talk to each other. With this exhibition and book, we have had the opportunity to show that writing and typographic design not only talk, but understand and collaborate and create with each other.

The original idea for the project came out of a conversation to discuss the involvement of 26 in the 2004 London Design Festival. 26 is a not-for-profit group launched in 2003 to inspire a greater love of words in business and the wider community. The conversation between John Simmons of 26 and Lynne Dobney of the London Design Festival led to the idea of pairing writers and designers to create twenty-six posters based on the individual letters of the alphabet. This seemed an exciting idea, with the potential to inspire groundbreaking work.

Lynne proposed that 26 should partner with the International Society of Typographic Designers, who had already expressed interest in mounting a typographic exhibition during the festival. So a meeting was arranged and, as was to become the way throughout this project, the idea met with an enthusiastic response. Freda Sack of the ISTD agreed to approach twenty-six designers to gain their commitment.

Within days, we had two lists: twenty-six writers and twenty-six typographers. The writers came breathlessly rushing, in the spirit of James Joyce, going "Yes yes yes." The idea of exploring language through an individual letter was immediately attractive to the writers and typographers. Both parties responded to the creative simplicity of the idea and the opportunity to work together to show their shared love of words.

By this point the British Library had been introduced as an additional partner. This was another stimulating development, giving us an exhibition venue and a source of inspiration for the teams working on the posters. The British Library offers an extraordinary space, but for too many it is an unknown or unexplored space. Here was the means to demonstrate the creative potential of its resources and open it up to new audiences. The British Library contains the world's knowledge in its collections of books, manuscripts, sound recordings, newspapers, stamps, patents and electronic media. Where better to explore the alphabet, the building blocks of knowledge?

The British Library believed that this could be more than a conventional exhibition. Although accustomed to curating archive materials, its staff were keen to break away from any thought of confining the exhibition to a single gallery. Indeed, they wanted to present something of a treasure trail, with posters of different formats, sizes and media located in many parts of the library: not just the impressive foyer space and galleries, but some of the more out-of-the-way areas. This gave an extra dimension to the brief we formulated for the twenty-six pairs.

By now they *were* pairs. Both 26 and ISTD had independently come up with a list of twenty-six members and assigned a letter to each. The two lists were then put together, so the pairing of writer and designer was decided randomly. The first each writer or designer knew about the partner they had been allocated was when they received the brief. At that point we all realized what an exciting collection of people had been gathered: writers from many different backgrounds, designers with the broadest range of typographic approaches, eminent names as well as those at early stages of their creative careers.

We deliberately kept the brief open. Although our expectation was that the writer would contribute words and the typographer would be concerned with design, we knew that each would stray into the other's thinking. Indeed, that's what we wanted to happen. That would be a more interesting creative process, and we hoped through this project to shed light on the nature of creativity between words and images.

Some of the partnerships would have to develop unconventional ways to collaborate. Many of the pairs would find it easy to come together if they were based near each other (particularly in London). But some of 26's writers were in remoter parts of the country, including Scotland. How would they link with their design partners – by phone, post, email? And some of the ISTD's designers were in other countries – Germany, the USA, the Netherlands. How would they establish working relationships in such a short time, in some cases never even meeting?

The individual letter was the starting point and focus. What does A mean to you? Or B? And on through the alphabet to Z? We believed a letter might suggest a story, a poem, a line or a series of thoughts. How would these thoughts translate into the visual medium of a typographic poster? We set no limits to the size of the posters (other than a minimum size of A0). The British Library is *big*. Would any pair want to take advantage of its sheer scale? If so, how would they deal with the challenge of producing the poster? For we had no production facility laid on for the teams; it was up to each pair to find a way to get their poster produced. In fact, as the project developed, a number of the works-in-progress were clearly moving well beyond the definition of a poster, and we were happy to keep conventional limitations out of the way. The teams experimented with formats and materials, and looked for inventive ways to display their thoughts.

The biggest constraint we gave people was time. We issued the brief in May 2004 and the London Design Festival was in September, so we needed completed artwork by the end of July. That was no time at all for teams to come together, explore and develop ideas, and produce their pieces for display in the library. But deadlines are part of the everyday life of all the participants.

The resources of the British Library were available to everyone. As a distinct bonus, all participants were given a reader's card to encourage research. We were invited one morning to a briefing session at which we were introduced to the library and given information about how to use its riches. In the lecture hall we were treated to a talk by Michelle Brown, curator of illuminated manuscripts. Her passion for and deep knowledge of her subject shone out.

This book documents what happened next. It looks at how the teams transformed the brief and the background information into twenty-six works to be displayed at the British Library. The process of making the works led to twenty-six contrasting stories. We always believed that the stories would have a value, as well as the works themselves. So we asked each team to record a diary of their collaboration. You can read these stories to understand the sometimes winding journeys to the final pieces. The creative process is seldom straightforward. As with the main brief, the diary brief set few limitations in terms of style, and the variety of approaches taken in the entries is interesting in itself.

BRITISH LIBRARY

At the end of it all, what did we find? We reinforced our belief that writing and typographic design are natural partners. We discovered afresh that creativity is inspired by words – and even by the individual letters that we use to make words. The project goes to the root of the way that people have explored their humanity throughout history. In the beginning was the word, and soon after that came the symbols, marks, hieroglyphs and letters that enabled us to transmit words beyond our own time. The British Library is a living testament to this idea.

We reaffirmed too that typography is a sophisticated form of communication, conveying purpose, emotion, atmosphere and hierarchy of information. From this limited set of twenty-six abstract shapes, good typographers use their craft to communicate the widest range of messages. From the writer's viewpoint too, this was a discovery (or rediscovery) of typography's potential to deepen the meaning of words. It was a pleasant surprise when Freda Sack quoted words that John Simmons had written in an earlier book, but forgotten:

"We should all care about what the words say – they are most powerful when the visual and the verbal combine...it's all about engaging with the thoughts and emotions of others, using verbal *and* visual means. Typography can be the bridge between the two."

This book is a visible demonstration of the positive relationship that exists between writers and typographers. Writers care about the way their words are read, and they get excited by the added dimension that good typography brings. Typographers understand the potential of language; they work with words constantly to realize that potential through design. This is a natural and powerful partnership, illustrated by the exhibition and this book.

Acknowledgements

From Freda Sack, ISTD

Thanks to:
Dian Hulse and Stuart de Rozario at Foundry Types whose help and support on this project have been invaluable.

All at Grade Design, who together with Peter Dawson have contributed so much.

Caroline Roberts for advice and always being there.

Most of all to the designers and writers themselves, and the printers, signmakers and suppliers who have been involved with the production of the posters.

I don't think anybody realizes the amount of time and energy expended by the designers, fuelled by their passionate involvement in typography – all for love...

Thanks to all these amazing people for making it happen.

From John Simmons, 26

All books are collaborative efforts. This book is even more so – at least twenty-six times more so. It will be impossible to acknowledge all the many people involved in the creation of this book and the exhibition that was its reason for being. I apologize that I'm unable to mention everyone by name.

First, many thanks to Lynne Dobney and the London Design Festival. The festival, founded by John Sorrell, has supported 26 since its launch; and Lynne has been a personal friend as well as a believer in 26 and ISTD.

Thanks to all my colleagues and contributors from 26 and ISTD. Their enthusiasm and brilliance are evident in these pages. As well as those who took direct part in the project, Ben Afia and Olivia Sprinkel were fantastic project managers. In addition to their involvement in creating works for the exhibition and the book, Tim Rich (O) and Tom Lynham (E) were enthusiastic and skilful keepers of the words; this book is so much better for their comments and insights. And Margaret Oscar (Y) whipped us all into shape.

The ISTD is a wonderful organization and it has been brilliantly represented by Freda Sack. Peter Dawson has contributed well beyond the call of duty, designing not only a poster (U) but every detail of this book with his colleagues at Grade Design. The 26 writers now have an enhanced appreciation of the power of typography.

The 26 works were made possible by the generosity and craft of many different people and companies who effectively sponsored their production. This book is another example of such generosity, beautifully printed by Good News Press.

I have known the British Library for some years, but have got to know it better through this project. The library is one of the world's treasures, but it is much more than its collections and buildings; it has wonderful people, among whom Carol Meads and Alan Sterenberg have been particularly good to work with. All the participants from 26 and ISTD were proud to have been invited into the British Library in this unique way, and our special thanks go to its chairman, Lord Eatwell.

Finally, thanks to Cyan Books, in particular Martin Liu and Pom Somkabcharti. Martin was an original member of 26. Cyan's approach demonstrates the publisher's belief in the creative partnership between writing and design, and this book is the perfect example.

Aa

Roger Fawcett-Tang + Sean Lewis

Sean's diary

The letter A gave Roger and me an advantage. It meant we were first. That suits me down to the ground. I like to be in at the start of new things.

Unlike many people in this book, I don't actually write for a living. However, I do look at whether there are robust concepts behind things. So I asked the question: does the letter A really confer an advantage? Well, you just have to flick through Yellow Pages to find the answer. You'll discover a myriad of companies that have adopted the letter to get ahead of the pack. A1 Plumbing, AA Appointments Limited, A Craftsmans Workshop, AAA Specialist Couriers, A & A Painters & Decorators... I would like to congratulate these companies and others like them for seizing that commercial advantage.

I would also hazard a guess that the main reason for you reading this diary piece is that it appears first in the book. Why haven't you flicked straight to L, P, Q or Y?

For something so small, the letter A is enormously important. It's a letter that leads. It has a tail that invites the rest of the alphabet to follow. A is so canny, it even makes a word on its own.

"Alphabet" itself begins with the letter A. Which isn't all that surprising, as the word is derived from the first two characters of the Greek alphabet, alpha and beta, which themselves derive from the first two characters of the Hebrew alphabet, aleph and bet. The quiet supremacy of the letter A is proved by the fact that it has stood the test of time and continues to lead the pack even after relative newcomers J, U, W, Y and Z have muscled their way into the alphabet.

While pulling together my thoughts on the letter A, I explored whether it's best represented at the end of things, rather than at the beginning. After all, the word Armageddon begins with A, and you can't get any more final than that. Even so, A has more associations with Adam than Armageddon. It's a positive letter, and its true distinctiveness is that it's at the beginning, not the end.

I feel Roger has interpreted some of my initial thoughts on the letter A into a considered typographic execution. A-class, in fact.

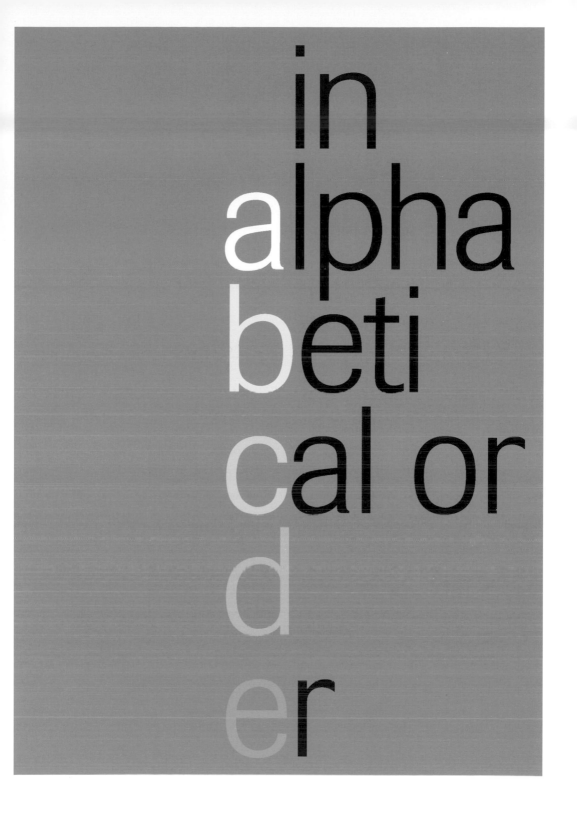

in alphabetical order

Designer: Roger Fawcett-Tang
Roger set up Struktur Design together with his wife Sanne in 1996, and divides his time between its offices in London and Århus, Denmark. He has written four books on graphic design: *Experimental Formats, Mapping, New Book Design* and *Experimental Formats 2*.

Writer: Sean Lewis
My personal profile (courtesy of my wife Alex):
Sean is
able, accessible, accountable, an achiever, an ad-libber, adept, aesthetic, ambitious, animated, appreciative, artistic, aspirational, assertive, amorous and sometimes annoying.

Sean isn't
affluent, airy-fairy, alarmist, aloof, anal, angelic, anonymous, antisocial, asphyxiating, athletic, average, awkward, an American, anchovy, android or anorak, and certainly not available!

Like all talented graphic designers, he has taken a raw idea and converted it into a clear, concise communication. I'm only sorry Roger and I didn't get to meet in person through this project. Our frenetic schedules wouldn't allow it. Thank heavens for email – an @ partnership – there's that letter again!

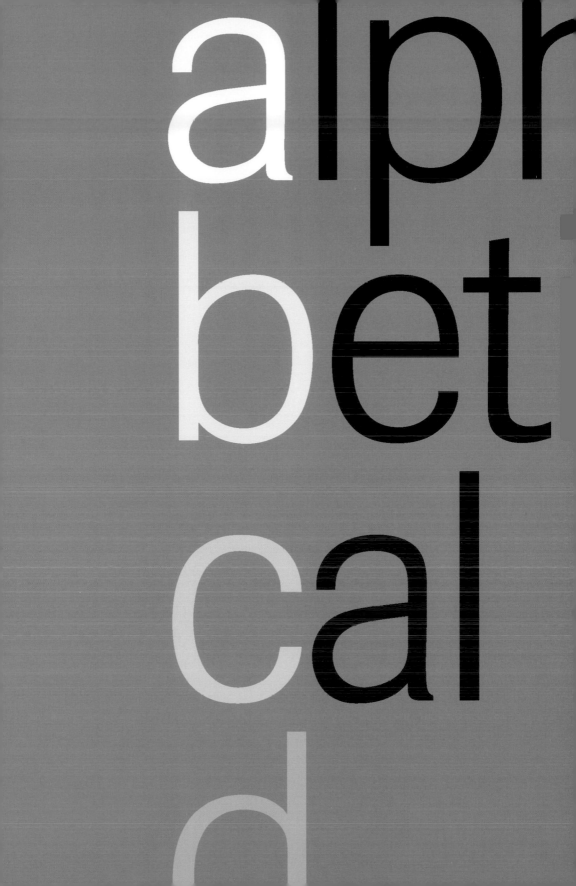

alph
bet
cal
d

Bb

Christine Fent + Mark Fiddes

Mark's diary

From *Schott's Original Miscellany* to the *Fortune* 500, our appetite for lists is insatiable, particularly those that chart the tumbling fortunes of celebrity.

The A-list "personality" is unimpeachable. For those C-listed, there awaits a certain swaggering notoriety. So pity the B-list, damned by the faintest of praise.

Yet at the heart of every list surely lies our need to make sense of the world, to impose order and scale. Just like a library. Which is where we started with our own B list for the British Library.

Oddly, this list was how Christine and I broke the ice on our first meeting. We realized how many of our heroes began with B. No other letter came close. Very quickly, our collection grew into a pantheon of those who have rocked our worlds. It was as if B people shared a powerful secret.

Despite our surnames both beginning with the uncompromising and spiky F, we were already suffering from B-ness envy. As for those double-blessed with Bs, we were awestruck. Think Brigitte Bardot, Bertolt Brecht.

But we stopped short of numerically ordering our top fifty Bs. We wanted visitors to do that for us, interactively, democratically. If they used their mobiles to text through their favourite Bs from the list, we would help highlight the British Library's commitment to clicks as well as mortar. (And we know how important the twenty-first century is to the library.)

There were, naturally, a number of other ideas in play. Suffice to mention one here.

Because the exhibition has been planned through 26, an organization pledged to improve the standards of business writing, we toyed with the concept of "B is for body copy."

The following short story explains why a rather grumpy Almighty created body copy. It would have made for a terrible poster layout. It really belongs in a book like this one.

The B-List

001 Brown J.
002 Beethoven v.L.
003 Beardsley P.
004 Bergmann I.
005 Bergmann I.
006 Beuys J.
008 Blake W.
009 Bach J.S.
010 Brando M.
011 Brecht B.
012 Björk
013 Böll H.
014 Botham I.
015 Borges J.L.
016 Bourgeois L.
017 Beckmann M.
018 Bowie D.
019 Byron G.
020 Best G.
021 Brontë E. and C.
022 Barthes R.
023 B Agnes
024 Bellow S.
025 Bill M.
026 Bernstein L.
027 Bogart H.
028 Bacall L.
029 Balzac H.
030 Bacon F.
031 Brancusi C.
032 Benn T.
033 Batman
034 Bardot B.
035 Bentham J.
036 Buddha
037 Bannister R.
038 Botticelli A.
039 Boadicia
040 Brandt B.
041 Bukowski C.
042 Bartok B.
043 Beckham D.
044 Branson R.
045 Brubeck D.
046 Basquiat J.-M.
047 Brahms J.
048 Berkeley G.
049 Baker C.
050 Baker J.
007 Bond 'J. Bond'

The B-List was compiled in a completely unscientific way and represents only the passions and prejudices of the authors. Any sense of historical or cultural authority derives entirely from this poster's position in the British Library.

Nevertheless, if you want to vote for the person you would like to top the all-time B-List, you can use your phone. Simply text BLIST and the code number to 82222. For example, to vote for James Bond, just text BLIST 007 to 82222. Votes cost 25p plus standard network charge. All proceeds are donated to the British Library Adopt a Book programme. For an update on the rankings go to www.theblist.net.

Massive thanks to Filter for their interactive genius and support.

Why B is for body copy

In the beginning was the Word, and the Word was with God, and the Word was God.

All of which had the smack of firm management and was just how He liked to run Creation. Everything was in its proper place, heavens and firmament, man and woman, even Eden.

Sooner or later, it all had to go pear-shaped.

More fool Him for planting knowledge in the shape of a fruit tree. Had He set it crawling upon the earth as a stag beetle, good and evil would have been consigned to a dusty shelf in the etymology dept.

But it is easy to be omniscient after the event.

"The serpent beguiled me," said Eve, adjusting her Gucci figleaf, "and I ate."

Yet God knew what was at the root of His daughter's eating disorder. The Word. He no longer had exclusive rights to it. "Behold," he said, "the man has become like us, knowing good and evil." With this he threw down his putter and stomped back to the clubhouse.

Before you could say Shadrach, Meshach, Abednego, Attorneys-at-Law, there were Words hopping all over Existence: little furry bundles of meaning, all breeding like rabbits. Millennia rolled by. God attempted a few metaphysical body-slams on Words, but the Babel incident only complicated the problem. Worse still, His only Son developed a gift for Words that made people like him even more.

Then along came advertising.

Ever since the serpent had first headlined the benefits of Eden-fresh produce to Eve, the persuasive power of advertising had been everywhere, from manhole covers to pub toilets. It got God to thinking.

"Behold! Advertising. Here in the print of press ads, brochures, annual reports and websites, I will entomb Words by the billion. Yeah, let Words slumber in cold grey columns for eternity, unread by anyone." With a whoop of poetic justice, He drained his vodka martini and returned to the throng outside.

"Ladies and gentlemen of the press," he announced, "it gives me divine pleasure to present to you a small improvement to the world. Please feel free to use it to bury any inconvenient facts or useless knowledge. It is called body copy. I thank you."

Designer: Christine Fent
Christine works as a designer and typographer in Bloomsbury. She has recently been invited to judge the Best International Book Design and the Design Austria awards.

Writer: Mark Fiddes
Mark is creative director of integration at Euro RSCG Worldwide. He serves on the Havas Creative Council and regularly judges at the Cannes Lions Awards. He lives in Wandsworth, London with Maribel, Alec and Sergi.

A final word on creative collaboration and what we learned, or rather confirmed.

1 Copywriters and typographers love working directly with each other because they have words in common.
2 The Marlborough Arms in Torrington Place offers an excellent Sauvignon Blanc for £3.25 a glass.
3 Robust ideas work across new and old media. Special thanks to Al Scott at Filter for his fizz and pioneering knowhow.

The B-List

001 Brown J.

002 Beethoven v.L.

003 Beardsley P.

Cc

Morag Myerscough + Charlotte Rawlins

Charlotte's diary

One of the first pieces of writing I came across when I googled the letter C was an article by a chap called Jakob Nielsen. "The letter 'C' is 95% bad," says Nielsen, who was struck by the letter's basic lack of function in the English language. "The sheer uselessness of a letter which just mimics the sound of not one but two different consonants is staggering." Nielsen goes on to discuss phasing out C altogether and replacing it with K and S.

If C is redundant because it can be replaced by the hard K and the soft S, isn't it equally interesting for the same reason? C is a chameleon, a letter of contrast: hard and soft sounds, positive and negative meanings, beginnings (creation), centres (middle C) and ends (A, B, C). Patterns start to emerge from C, with one of the strongest being its polarities.

Morag and I met for the first time on Thursday 3 June at Morag's studio in Clerkenwell. We quickly found that we have our own polar Cs – my soft Charlotte and Morag's spiky middle name, Crichton – and this seemed auspicious. So we had our starting point. We also agreed straight away that our piece about C should say something about us as individuals; neither of us wanted to follow an objective scientific investigation (after all, that might leave us in Mr Nielsen's kamp, declaring our subject obsolete and effectively doing ourselves out of a job).

We thought about our own ways of working and how we would approach this kind of exercise. Both of us are used to working in a democratic way. Morag often kicks off a project by getting together with all the parties involved to define a brief. Similarly, as a brand manager with the responsibility to define the brand in the first instance, but also to adapt to the requirements of different users, I always need to solicit different views and negotiate consensus.

So we thought a good place to go next would be to canvass opinions on C among our friends and colleagues. An email went out to 50 of them and their responses immediately flooded back. Once again, the first constant was the presence of contrast and extremes. To see, the sea, bright blue, sunshine, vitamin C and vivid oranges and yellows on the one hand; the congestion zone and the dreaded grade C on the other. In among all these associations, the other constant was the C word.

Designer: Morag Myerscough
I approach every project without preconceived ideas. I believe the role of design is to perform as an integral part of the environment it is in. It should engage directly with its surroundings and convey information to be experienced, rather than just seen.

Writer: Charlotte Rawlins
Although, sadly, no one pays me to be a writer, I currently work in branding and communications which, happily, give me plenty of opportunity for wordplay. And while we're at it, my favourite word is serendipity.

Our next meeting was the first real meeting of minds and, we're not ashamed to say, it occurred at the lowest of lowbrow levels. I arrived to find the wall of Morag's studio papered with variations on the theme of the word "cunt." We had cunt, kunt and various puns ranging from "C U next Tuesday" to "Has anybody seen Mike Hunt?" And there it was – the pieces fell into place. C, after all, is almost unique in having its own word. The C word. The hardest word of them all. In fact, there's only one other letter that has its own word and that's F… but no one's that scared of using the F word these days.

Why is it such a bad word? We're not going to turn this into an etymological exploration of the origins of cunt, but in brief, the word dates back to Middle English and originally just signified the female genitalia. Its evolution into a term of abuse is relatively recent – probably only occurring in the twentieth century – but it has managed to storm into the lead as pretty much the worst thing you can say to anyone. Yet funnily enough many people seem to have a soft spot for the C word, the last bastion of real naughtiness in the English language, and so among all the beautiful bright images of the sun, sea and vitamin C, most people just had to sneak it in when they were asked to think of C.

We couldn't resist making this our subject; in fact, it became a game of chicken as we waited to see who would back down first. And neither of us did. So, as two fairly soft, feminine types, we agreed that our presentation of the C word would be our best illustration and expression of the soft and hard extremes of C. Morag and Charlotte bring you "Has anybody seen Mike Hunt?" – a lads' gag played out by women. To play further with the male–female and soft–hard theme, we've chosen to style our lads' gag in a soft pink subversion of a neon girlie-show sign.

The use of the pun will, we hope, avoid offending the gentler sensibilities of the British Library reader. Our aim isn't to shock, it's just to have a bit of fun with our letter and to say that we don't think the C word is such a bad word after all. It's the hardest of Cs, but it's brought to you by us in the gentlest way we could think of – not really featuring it at all, just getting you to say it to yourselves and helping you to have a little smile with us along the way.

Has any

Mike

ody seen

unt?

Dd

David Quay + Gordon Kerr

david's diary

we started working together very easily after our introductory emails. gordon sent me a list of ideas he thought appropriate for me to comment on. many seemed too wordy for a poster that has to stand out in the vast entrance space of the british library and i did remind him of this. one of his ideas i thought had possibilities but i detected his lack of enthusiasm for all of them. after a few more emails i received one that said:

"ok david. i'm now sorted. none of the things i have been working on and thinking about are really me. what i am is a poet – book published in the states last year – and that is how i should express myself in this project. it's what feels right to me. so, have been spending the weekend working on a sonnet, a love poem basically which quite simply has a punchline which features the letter in question. that is what i want to do and what i feel happiest with. there will be lots for you to play with in it and hopefully there won't be too many poems in the final works."

i was taken aback. a love sonnet for god's sake, what the hell can i do with a love sonnet? who does he think he is? does he expect something set in bembo? i was floored and i made a few attempts at translating the poem in a sympathetic and traditional way. nothing worked and i felt worried for two days and kept thinking, "can i solve this?"

in the end i sent him an email expressing my views:

"i am working on your text, thinking about a sympathetic treatment. should it be in bembo, garamond or caslon, or a poetic script? no that is definitely not me, i am a hardline modernist (i am not that hard but i thought he would understand where i was coming from better) so i abandoned what I was doing and started afresh. it is now going well."

i also suggested that we meet up the following monday as i was in london that week, to which i received the reply:

"that would be terrific. it's a date. and hard, uncompromising modernism set against a lyrical sonnet would be a fantastic clash. i like it. see you monday."

this gave me three pleasant days to resolve the design. we met and had tea together. we warmed to each other immediately. i showed him the theme i had been working on and various

once, summer nights, perfumed by rain,
would tease love's syntax from her lips,
like a single thread from out the skein,
a breath caught deep, between the sips.
but her silence now does love oppugn
and the slighted heart down cast,
stark midnight geese correct the moon
and each kiss brings us closer to the last.

rain falls in exclamation marks,
but nothing more may i promise her.
love's ardour is set, in the fading dark,
like mercury, in a cold thermometer.

now love's present can no longer be,
with the addition of just one letter – 'd'.

the letter d

writer gordon kerr
designer david quay

possibilities and variations. his response was very positive and immediate: "that one," which was the most hard-edged of all my ideas. we were both satisfied, we had achieved an unexpected harmony and melding of disparate expressions.

Gordon's diary

"Endings are elusive, middles are nowhere to be found, but worst of all is to begin, to begin, to begin."

I bet the guy who said that, the American writer Donald Barthelme, didn't start a new business and a new life and find himself walking with a stick as he tried to begin, though.

The project was put to me in the very week that I was launching an entirely new career and an entirely new lifestyle after 30 years of wage slavery. I was flattered.

The letter D. *Dawdle, dilatory, delay, defer* – my letter was rich with the right language for a dilettante such as me. This was my kind of letter! But I was busy, trying to organize an increasingly complex life. I put it to one side for a few weeks. My design partner David Quay seemed relaxed about it. We had lots of time, after all.

Then, one Wednesday in mid-June, as I began to smell the sweet scent of deadline adrenalin, I awoke in the throes of a sciatic trauma in which all the nerves of my left leg short-circuited and my back became the focus of a pain that went to a place beyond pain. The next few weeks are something of a blank from which I eventually emerged having to use a walking stick.

Of course, while incapacitated, I thought about the project. I had ideas and I put them to my partner. A children's story: David had originally suggested it in one of our infrequent phone calls. The letter D could be kidnapped by the nasty letters at the end of the alphabet, X, Y and Z, that only get to be in pointless words like xylophone or zebra. I also thought about definitions of words that could mean something else (describe: to sack a writer; debunk: to get out of bed... I know, sadly, not many get it). I thought up a story in which the letter D resigns from the alphabet, but the wonderful website The Onion had beaten me to it with a hilarious piece about a letter that withdraws from the Sesame Street alphabet following the announcement that a homosexual Muppet is to join the cast.

Designer: David Quay
Ravensbourne School of Art & Design, aka "Bromley Bauhaus."
Speciality: lettering design and pure graphics.
1989: started The Foundry type design studio with Freda Sack.
Teaches regularly internationally.
Now lives in Amsterdam, designing mainly typefaces.

Writer: Gordon Kerr
Poet, writer and marketeer; after twenty years with Oddbins, Waterstone's and Bloomsbury, Gordon has set up his own company, Vox, to give voice to others' initiatives as well as to pursue his own writing projects.

Time was passing. What to do about this letter?

An important letter, too. The fourth letter of the alphabet, corresponding to the Greek delta, the usual symbol for a voiced dental. Capital D represents a note in the musical scale and in Roman numerals the number 500. An upper case delta is used for large or macroscopic changes, and a lower-case delta for small or microscopic changes. And so on.

So of course I wrote a sonnet.

"A bloody sonnet!" as my ever-patient design partner described it. But I thought: I want to produce something that is from *me*. Not a piece of research, not a historical document. I write poems. I've even been published. And I was proud of my poem. Like most modern poets, I rarely write anything that rhymes and the discipline of the sonnet was truly challenging. It is a love poem and deals with the fact that the simple addition of the letter D to the word "love" can cast it into the past. The language used is deliberately archaic in places and, as I found, the whole poem contrasts with the strikingly modern approach that David Quay adopted in his beautifully simple design. David is a type designer, and a very good one too. His design is true to what he is about and I think that is what I like about what we have produced. It is personal and it is beautiful.

We met, finally, David and I, and, after showing me his various design options, we shared our histories. He told me of his life in Amsterdam, drinking coffee with the goldsmith in the flat beneath his in the mornings and cycling out into the Dutch countryside, under those huge skies borrowed from Jan van Goyen and Jacob van Ruisdael, in the afternoons. And then working into the night, crafting his fonts. It sounded idyllic, as other people's lives often do.

Perhaps, after all, that is what a project like this is all about. Learning the stories that go into making another person and producing something beautiful along the way.

Ee

Lucienne Roberts + Tom Lynham

Lucienne Roberts: The agony

Graphics isn't graphics without a client. Love them or loathe them, their need defines the process, giving it meaning and structure. Because (and I know it's a cliché) they have a problem to be solved, everyone involved works to achieve a common objective.

Tom and I struggled to find a shared goal. We met. We discussed politics and the divisiveness of London house prices. We agreed about Thatcher. But it wasn't enough. We were forced to be each other's client.

I wondered if the prevalence of the hard-working letter E could be used as some kind of political metaphor, or whether "E is for ego" might be a starting point. Tom thought we couldn't ignore the fact that E has come to have an extremely powerful meaning all of its own. He researched the brand names for Ecstasy and proposed listing them as a means to unsettle and provoke debate. For me the message was worryingly ambiguous. "I can't do anything that could be misconstrued as an endorsement, or worse still act as an advertisement," I explained. I agonized.

I take the responsibility of the graphic designer very seriously. A client has a message; they employ us to help convey it. Are we happy to endorse this message, to give it more power, to help it travel further? I was faced with the sort of dilemma I expect to encounter in commercial practice, but with a delightfully egocentric twist. Should I bow out or would this be undervaluing my role as a graphic designer?

I sent an email. I didn't want Tom to feel the onus was on him but equally I didn't want to appear to usurp or take control. Tom graciously came back with another suggestion: to use the periodic table of elements as a basis for a periodic table of the emotions. Lovely idea, and it's all about grid structures and surely has to be in Helvetica. What more could a girl want?

I approach typography like a faux science so I set about trying to understand the periodic table. Why is it the shape it is? What are the relationships between horizontal and vertical elements? What do all those numbers mean? But as I tried to impose structure, Tom gently resisted.

We both use the word "pure" to describe ideas and processes. Tom wanted to retain the purity of the table but to insert new

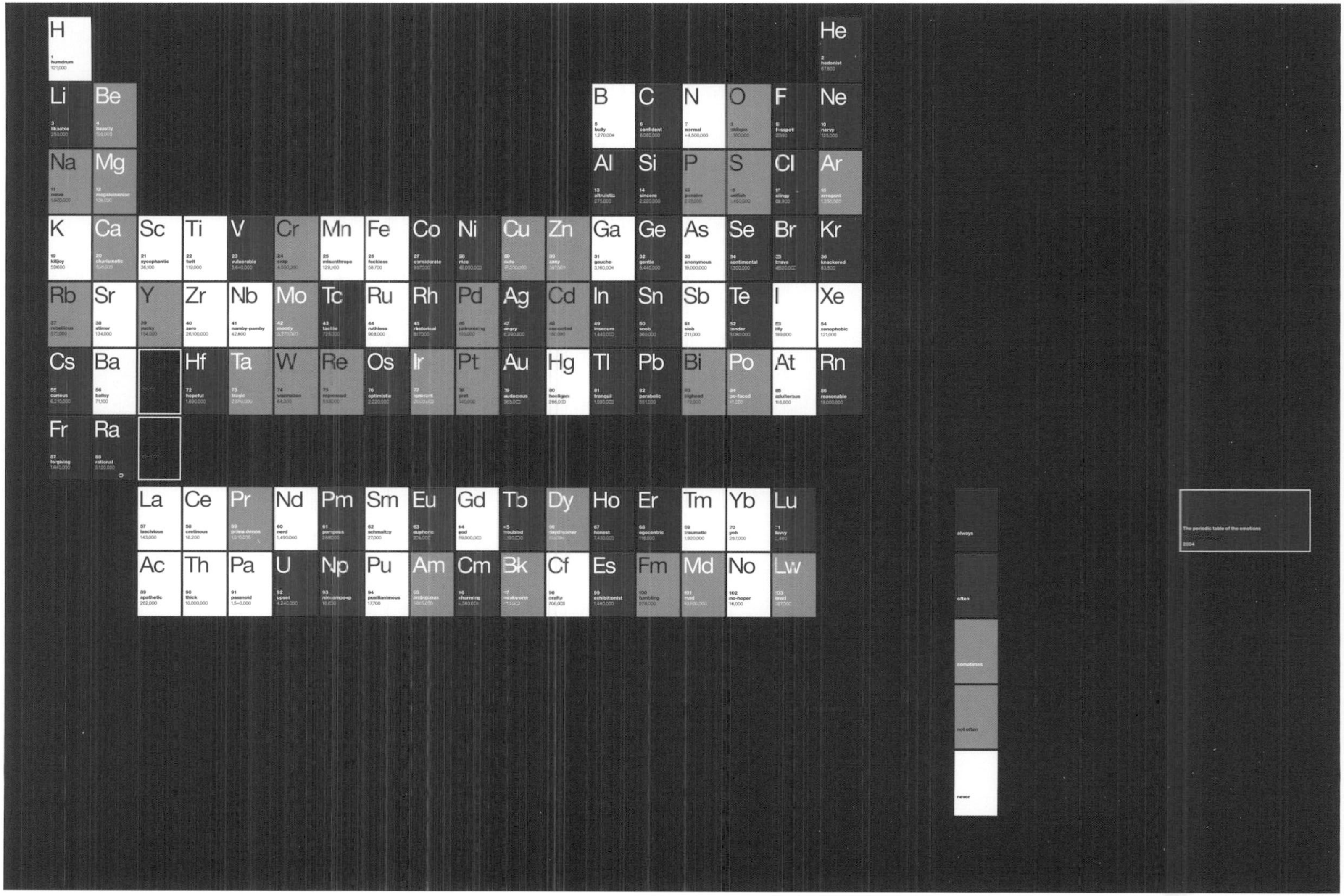

Symbol	No.	Emotion	Figure
H	1	humdrum	121,000
He	2	hedonist	67,800
Li	3	likeable	250,000
Be	4	beastly	[illegible]
B	5	bully	1,270,000
C	6	confident	6,080,000
N	7	normal	44,500,000
O	8	oblique	[illegible]
F	9	fusspot	[illegible]
Ne	10	nervy	125,000
Na	11	naive	[illegible]
Mg	12	megalomaniac	[illegible]
Al	13	altruistic	275,000
Si	14	sincere	2,220,000
P	15	pensive	[illegible]
S	16	selfish	[illegible]
Cl	17	clingy	[illegible]
Ar	18	arrogant	[illegible]
K	19	killjoy	59,600
Ca	20	charismatic	[illegible]
Sc	21	sycophantic	36,100
Ti	22	twit	119,000
V	23	vulnerable	5,640,000
Cr	24	crap	[illegible]
Mn	25	misanthrope	129,000
Fe	26	feckless	58,700
Co	27	considerate	[illegible]
Ni	28	nice	42,000,000
Cu	29	cute	[illegible]
Zn	30	zany	[illegible]
Ga	31	gauche	3,160,000
Ge	32	gentle	5,440,000
As	33	anonymous	19,000,000
Se	34	sentimental	[illegible]
Br	35	brave	[illegible]
Kr	36	knackered	83,500
Rb	37	rebellious	[illegible]
Sr	38	stirrer	134,000
Y	39	yucky	154,000
Zr	40	zero	28,100,000
Nb	41	namby-pamby	42,800
Mo	42	moody	[illegible]
Tc	43	tactile	[illegible]
Ru	44	ruthless	908,000
Rh	45	rhetorical	[illegible]
Pd	46	patronising	[illegible]
Ag	47	angry	[illegible]
Cd	48	conceited	[illegible]
In	49	insecure	1,440,000
Sn	50	snob	360,000
Sb	51	slob	211,000
Te	52	tender	[illegible]
I	53	iffy	[illegible]
Xe	54	xenophobic	121,000
Cs	55	curious	6,210,000
Ba	56	ballsy	71,100
Hf	72	hopeful	1,890,000
Ta	73	tragic	[illegible]
W	74	[illegible]	[illegible]
Re	75	repressed	[illegible]
Os	76	optimistic	2,220,000
Ir	77	ignorant	[illegible]
Pt	78	prat	[illegible]
Au	79	audacious	[illegible]
Hg	80	hooligan	286,000
Tl	81	tranquil	1,090,000
Pb	82	parabolic	851,000
Bi	83	bighead	[illegible]
Po	84	po-faced	[illegible]
At	85	adulterous	116,000
Rn	86	reasonable	19,000,000
Fr	87	forgiving	[illegible]
Ra	88	rational	[illegible]
La	57	lascivious	143,000
Ce	58	cretinous	16,200
Pr	59	prima donna	[illegible]
Nd	60	nerd	1,490,000
Pm	61	pompous	[illegible]
Sm	62	schmaltzy	27,000
Eu	63	euphoric	[illegible]
Gd	64	god	[illegible]
Tb	65	troubled	[illegible]
Dy	66	daydreamer	[illegible]
Ho	67	honest	[illegible]
Er	68	egocentric	[illegible]
Tm	69	traumatic	1,920,000
Yb	70	yob	267,000
Lu	71	luvvy	[illegible]
Ac	89	apathetic	262,000
Th	90	thick	10,000,000
Pa	91	paranoid	[illegible]
U	92	upset	4,240,000
Np	93	nincompoop	[illegible]
Pu	94	pusillanimous	17,700
Am	95	ambiguous	[illegible]
Cm	96	charming	[illegible]
Bk	97	bookworm	[illegible]
Cf	98	crafty	706,000
Es	99	exhibitionist	1,480,000
Fm	100	fumbling	[illegible]
Md	101	mad	[illegible]
No	102	no-hoper	16,000
Lw	103	lewd	[illegible]

always

often

sometimes

not often

never

The periodic table of the emotions

2004

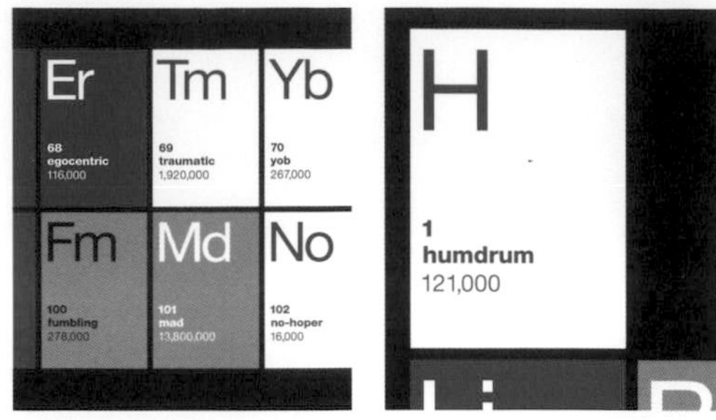

words and leave the decoding to the viewer. To me, an idea is pure when it is rigorously conceived, and so I struggled initially to apply a meaningful code.

I was reminded of the saying that a film is made three times: once when it is written (Tom), once when it is shot (me) and once when it is edited (the viewer). Tom sent a rich and multifarious list of alternative words to accompany each elemental symbol. I set about the delicious process of selection. Sometimes a word association made the choice immediately clear; sometimes an obviously foreign or ancient derivation appealed or a sound was simply too comical to resist. Having gone with this more subjective approach, I set about giving each word a numerical value and a form of colour coding. Putting each word into a Google search gave the numercial values – constantly changing but "God" and "nice" seem to fare pretty well. The colour coding emphasizes the different personal interpretations that are possible.

Although our poster has appropriated the visual language of science, it is unscientific. We used the 1964 version of the table. Just like this original, our table is open to additions with the added option of subtractions and reorderings. Most people see and use graphic design every day; it is fundamentally egalitarian. This simultaneously elevating and humbling aspect of design is what interests me. I don't want visitors to the British Library to assume our table has some rarified meaning. Essentially it is as playful or profound as each viewer chooses to make it.

Tom Lynham: The ecstasy

One of the really enticing things about this high-profile project is – no client. No client to umm & ahh over my p's & q's. No client terrified of a radical concept. No client rejecting adventurous writing. Ahhhh FREEDOM!

On our creative blind date, Lucie & I meet for tea at the Waterside Café in the Barbican. We ramble through design & designers, language & class, politics & semiotics and the legacies of Thatcherism. We carve out our criteria for the poster: bring fresh blood into the British Library, show how language is appropriated by new generations, reflect colliding cultures, deal with fundamental issues and enjoy the ride.

Designer: Lucienne Roberts
Lucienne Roberts set up the studio sans+baum in the late 1980s, aiming to ally her commitment to modernist typography with a socialist agenda. Clients have ranged from health-related charities to galleries and publishers, and include the Institute of Cancer Research, the Hayward Gallery and the British Council.

Writer: Tom Lynham
Creative thinking and the origination of ideas drive Tom's work in written and visual communications. He helps clients discover how compelling language and charismatic behaviours can trigger wonderful chemistries with their audiences. His clients include WWF, Barclays Bank, Sainsbury's, Boots, BT and Survival International.

Back at the studio I begin wordstorming E. Some ideas prosaic, others abstract. But a little voice inside my head insists that E = Ecstasy. It's the only letter of the alphabet that stands for an entire culture. It's consumed in vast quantities, yet we have no idea of the long-term consequences. Ecstasy tablets are branded with names that reflect many aspects of our lives. Searches in the British Library and on the internet yield an incredible diversity. Alice in Wonderland meets Dennis the Menace. Roobarb & Custard rub shoulders with Rolls-Royce.

I email the list plus a watertight rationale to Lucie and look forward to her enthusiastic endorsement. I don't want our poster to be finger-wagging or judgemental. I want it simply to name the names and provoke debate. Lucie responds. She doesn't want to do it. She has very negative feelings about drugs but is prepared to talk it over. We negotiate a compromise in the Geffrye Museum café. Over the next days I try to include our personal perspectives but they dilute its brutish charm. Emails fly. Lucie offers to withdraw from the project. I consider finding another partner, but the essence of my work is to generate solutions that everyone can work with.

I bury Ecstasy and wander around the reading rooms, getting a sense of the space, pulling random books from shelves. The building groans with the ghosts of ideas, inventions, discoveries, theories and stories. I cast another E into the database and the periodic table of the elements bites. After the creative block it looks deliciously seductive. This is word heaven: 68 Er – erbium, 69 Tm – thulium, 70 Yb – ytterbium. I learn that the properties of 67 Ho – holmium are *soft, malleable* and *magnetic*. I know people like that. Can I hijack these physical ingredients and substitute a table of emotional elements? I hunt for character traits that could sit in the Ho box and find *horny, honest, horrid* and *hothead*. This is dynamite. E = emotion.

The next question is strategic. Can I find 103 human conditions that correspond to the acronyms in the table? Lucie loves the idea. She published a book about design grids and this is the mother of all grids. The creative high kicks in, better than any drug. And I am reminded of the reason I do this job.

Ff

Ben Parker & Paul Austin + Laura Forman

Laura's diary

If you ever need cheering up, give me a call and I'll show you the photo on my reader's pass. I look incredibly pleased to have joined the British Library. And that was before I found out about half the things they have there. The smile would be bigger now.

I knew that my letter was F. And I knew that I'd be working with Ben Parker and Paul Austin, founding partners of MadeThought. "First things first," I thought, already true to the F theme, "we should meet up." Right from the start, I wanted to respond to the brief with a poem. I love writing poetry and I'm fresh from a couple of Arvon Foundation courses earlier in the year. So I packed three or four poems and chatted with the taxi driver about the vicious Swiss cheese plant he used to have. Soon I was at MadeThought.

It was a great meeting.

Ben and Paul are good and kind and easy to talk to, which is important. I liked the feel of their pared-down design, the strength of their modernist approach with the occasional maverick element. Among other things, they showed me their innovative exhibition book for JAM: Tokyo–London at the Barbican and their logotype for MangaJo drinks. I browsed while they read. They seemed to like lots of the images in my poems. We approved of each other's work and decided that everything was going to be OK.

At that stage, I had a vague feeling that F could stand for "finding." After all, that's what you do at a library: you search, you find what you need, you learn. But I wanted to spend some time at the British Library, get to know it better, do some research.

I planned to go there one evening, after work. To get in the mood, I decided to look out for things starting with F. All day. On the Tube there was a crowd of faces looking back at me. There was a woman doing her make-up feature by feature. There was fiction: someone reading *A Room with a View*, a favourite of mine that brought Florence into the carriage. Then work was busy, so the other 25 letters were clamouring for a look-in as I worked on my writing projects at Interbrand. But the end of the day arrived and I headed for Covent Garden to get the tube up to the library. F was everywhere. It was weaving round legs wearing fishnets. When I got there, it was in the flags that flutter outside.

ISTD Typographers/ 26 Writers. Exhibition at The British Library.

Writer/ Laura Forman. Design/ MadeThought.

Ff.

When I was as tall as the book stack by my bed is now,
I'd push my finger along the pages,
Prodding each word to see if it had any life in it.
When I could call them all, they'd shake awake
And tell me a story.
I don't even notice it happening any more.

01

Facts just ride in cable cars that glide
Up thought wires between the page and my eyes.
They jump out at the top and head for my brain.
The wires loop round like escalator handrails,
Collecting more from the front of the queue that snakes
Round corners in well-ordered lines and paragraphs.

02

Soon I'll find the fact that changes everything.
A jewel that persuades me to set fire to my old notes,
Smelting fountain pen nibs and staples to create
A setting that gives it chance to shine.

03

04

Fact finding.

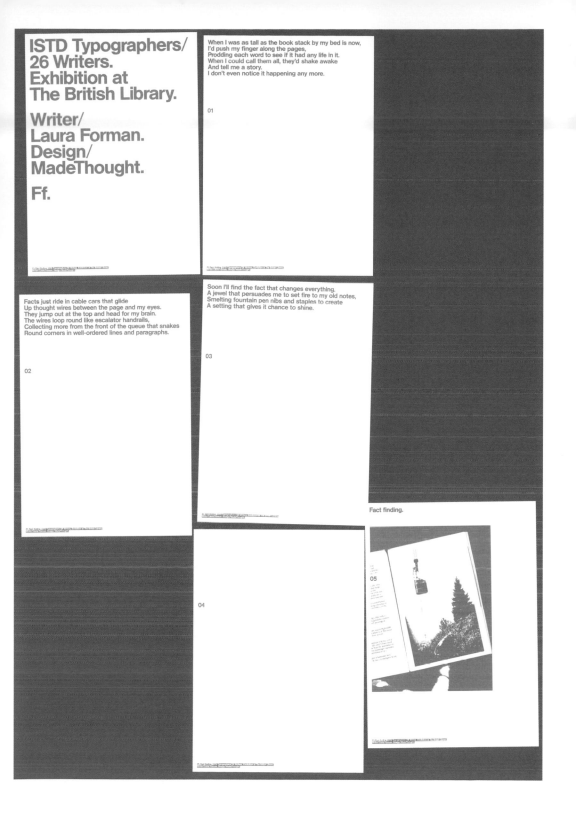

Designers: Ben Parker and Paul Austin
Ben Parker and Paul Austin founded MadeThought in 2000. They have completed many high-profile projects including the JAM: Tokyo–London exhibition book, the MTV Base channel identity and packaging for Stella McCartney's first fragrance. Current clients include Reiss, Nokia and Yves Saint Laurent.

I wasn't sure where to start. But I liked the Paolozzi statue of Newton in the piazza and thought I'd try a poem about that. The clouds were on fast-forward across the sky and the sun made my pen into a sundial. It was fun to write the poem but it didn't feel like the answer yet. I wandered into and wondered at one of the reading rooms: Rare Books and Music. Being in a library when you don't have anything specific to find out is odd. I made for the F section and saw a book about the composer Fauré, some of whose choral works I know. It was a life in letters, and that life was leaping from the page. Fauré joked that he felt truly famous when he saw a pair of boots for sale with a style named after him.

F was becoming too flexible, too feisty. There were so many things to choose from. I went back on a Saturday morning with a university friend to indulge in the answer to most problems: tea and cake. I can recommend the plum Danish pastries. I was taken with one of the quotes on the café wall: "Food is to eat, not to frame and hang on the wall." What about writing about food and hanging it on the wall?

I kept it at the back of my mind while we visited the exhibition galleries. If you haven't been yet, go. You can see music manuscripts handwritten by composers. The last page of Captain Scott's diary. Listen to the plainchant voice of W. B. Yeats intoning "The Lake Isle of Innisfree." See a first draft of one of Seamus Heaney's poems, complete with scribbled corrections. Original Beatles lyrics scrawled on paper napkins. Magna Carta.

It was uplifting, inspiring. I went home to work on my poem. It was partly about food and partly about the hunger for knowledge. It took a long time. It was a neat answer to the brief. That was probably the problem. When I went to talk about it with Ben and Paul at their new überchic offices near London Bridge, they seemed disappointed that it didn't have the same feel as the work I'd showed them at the outset. I'd edited myself out of it almost completely, and that's no good at all. But in a way, I was secretly glad. They could tell the difference between my real poetry and a poem I'd written with half an eye on an imaginary audience.

I went back to the drawing board, well, notebook, and decided that I preferred the theme of finding that had been nagging at me

Writer: Laura Forman
Laura Forman read natural sciences at Cambridge. She joined Interbrand in 2000 and is now their senior writer. She likes to write poems, read books, cook nice food and sing.

since the beginning. I wrote three or four poems, refusing to let on to myself which would be the one for the exhibition (though I did, of course, have a pretty good inkling). That way, I could write without all those readers-to-be staring at me.

The final poem is about a fact-finding mission at the library. But it starts early on in the story, with learning to read. I'll let you do the rest. I called Ben and Paul in a mood made from excitement and nervousness. I needed them to feel good about the poem, to want to work their design magic on it. They did.

Ff. Fact finding. ISTD Typographers/26 Writers. Exhibition at The British Library. Writer/Laura Forman. Design/MadeThought.

**Facts just ride in cable cars that glide
Up thought wires between the page and my eyes.
They jump out at the top and head for my brain.
The wires loop round like escalator handrails,
Collecting more from the front of the queue that snakes
Round corners in well-ordered lines and paragraphs.**

02

Gg

Nick Bell + Mark Griffiths

The benefit of being tall Nick Bell

Hi Mark **Tuesday 22 June 2004 6:49 PM**

I quite like the image of a vertiginous wall of text that a child could climb down using the g as footholds. That reminds me of walls I used to climb over to scrump apples – the orchard was an accidental discovery when climbing to retrieve a tennis ball. The wall was over 8 feet high and once I jumped off it… my chin hit my knee and I bit the end of my tongue off!

Hi Mark **Monday 5 July 4:15 PM**

What about producing a text that covers the poster in its entirety? Text size can be quite large. I can set it so that every letter g makes a path going up the poster.

We could change the letterforms so that every letter stroke carries the direction in which it is written like in those children's books we looked at. We could then end up with a new custom typeface that has arrowheads on all the downward strokes.

Our diary piece can mention how in Ladybird books, the letter g is drawn differently with an open jaw (instead of a loop) to make it easier for kids to read (and write), and how we see it as a leg-up into reading (and writing), as a climb into the alphabet. Ladybird books provided the footholds for children faced with the daunting task of learning to read. They were designed to make reading accessible.

Hi Mark **Thursday 22 July 11:30 AM**

Nice to speak with you on the phone just now, much better than emails. OK, so we agree that it would be better if the voice of the text is not that of a child but an adult. This allows the writing to be richer and sophisticated enough to cope with communicating the playful idea of reading the world as typography.

We have now established that the wall is the obstacle that stands for the difficulty of learning to read and write; that everything outside the garden (on this side of the wall) is wild; that the garden (on the other side of the wall) stands for wildness tamed; that the wild is by its nature hard to control (hard to read); that the garden stands for the bounty of knowledge accessible through reading and writing – a library.

getting into the garden is not easy. it's hidden by a wall that's higher than a giraffe. a giraffe looks like an h if it faces the right way but most of the time they don't. baboons could pass for daubed full stops if they squatted still for long enough and flying monkeys would be speech marks if they could freeze in mid air. when an ostrich sticks its head in the ground it makes a comma but only animators can make them do that. from the sloping back of a giraffe you can see the tops of the trees in the garden if you can cling on. the awkward way they walk makes that pretty impossible. better to use a trampoline: wall, garden lawn, wall, garden lawn, wall, squirrel on garden lawn, wall, garden lawn and so on. from great heights everything appears better organised. road junctions are crisp and geometric, the countryside looks manmade. only rivers disobey the rules which makes it easy to spot a canal: a silver needle pointing to the horizon. from up there you can see into the garden and make out its entrance by tracing its y-shaped drive: one branch winding to the front door, the other disappearing into the orchard. for the first time its secret corners can be opened, its stories read, now that garden begins with a g and not a g.

Designer: Nick Bell
Happy to leave the marketing of products and companies to others, Nick Bell devotes his time and passion to the content and design of those things that make life more interesting, like books, magazines and exhibitions.

Writer: Mark Griffiths
Mark Griffiths is an independent branding consultant and writer driven mad by the meaninglessness of marketing language. Recent author of *Guinness is Guinness*, he lives with his wife, teddy bears and goldfish in Shakespeare's shadow.

In the text an adult looks at animals, and like a child compares them to the shape of letters. But it is only inside the garden that all animals and plants spell out intelligible words and sentences.

Everything seems to make more sense when you are high up above looking down. We are using the bird's-eye view to stand for being older and wiser – how the ability to read gives you new perspective and how that can be expressed through the skill of writing. From up high it is possible to see into the garden. From a great height the world is like a map that can be read.

learning to read mark griffiths

sometimes i feel so gaga sometimes i feel so grr especially today may twentieth the day we meet the british library how do you meet a library and just how am i going to produce an arbitrary communication based on the letter g woke up at four fifteen with the shits those bloody mussels in birmingham last night miss my six fifty train to london its the british library or the toilet bowl no contest there text john to apologize he is full of enthusiasm for ancient manuscripts but i cant get illuminated by old things that old punk sense never leaves me not really interested in words just meaning as james joyce said language is such a secondary form of communication what came first nitpicking they say language is a form of grooming developed when distant ancestors found that congregating in large numbers made scratching the fleas from the hair of their immediate neighbours inconvenient if not impossible so language came and numbers too are a human construct and numerologists assign numbers to letters and some think numbers come closer to meaning than language hmmm and a is one and b is two and g is seven and seven is a mysterious number my name and birthdate together add up to seven hah and yes theres a name for this kind of figuring hidden meanings from the geometric shapes of letters and from the numerical values of words and of course gematria begins with g and that essential logic just proves numbers are a universal language because letters are symbols for sound and sound vibrates and creates form in order to know these rates of vibration we need numbers yes indeed so a letters numbered place in the alphabet is its rate of vibration when either thought or spoken

```
                                   .........,.,.
                              .,-;oc??crvjrlzrii?;,.                  .         .
                         .-?;?;vofzcnocrjj?r?;i????,.              ,i,      .;-
                       .,;-lnocclxovjnc&ucovt????v?u;.             ;n&-    .?r-
                      .;;utucstczov&ojjitc?iv;?;ivt?t?;.           j;oo;  rzlr
                     ,;?ijnjnzuoakinnczjl?v;i?i;rnljujv;          .r;g??c?zt?u.
                    ;l?u??jonjcn&seniu?i?;;;?;?uvfjonki          ?odawzv;;,-;?-
                   ,;?riinouzuekegyeyanr;;-;;j??ijxueds;.     ,jhgeollr;-,-;;
                 .-r?uf&ogswseaeeggggk?;;;;;??oc&eags?;     ?eek&aeulvijn?vir;
                 .;r;coozaykegskwhkurv?-?;;lrfankgsn?,   .ls?juc??,vwnvksl;?;..
                 .??iwvofsewcst?-;-?,?;??;?zuzeoghj?;. ?oojvsz?v???iuz&sz;;?,..
                 ,?czvzl??;,-.     ,,?;-;;;?rz&kw&sfn;?vnnr?ijnj;?rcossonsrcztu?- ..
                  .?;;,...        .,l;rlrtlnn&sykjeo;wehut?-;;?ixr?;l&kkoo?rhi;....
                                  .;;crc?cjcoeayeo&gsyeuctr?;;?r?;?r?;ckdenuzjtgz.
                              .-??;vztcnsefaeeeekeeytj?cn?--.-;ryo&geo?-;t??
                             ;.??ioosnjbf&eesorrno&&ojv?j?;;,-i;-;csemddt;;;;.
                             ;;ic;ufzsseekoxnv;?cuicww&nr?;;-;.i;?&kggyn?-?c,
                            .-;zu?fnnwwksoovt?;;;;?iau?tsu?i?;??lfggxj?,.;j.
                            ;??lnjsef&eot?;;?;tlric?;?;?iucojozsksw;;tv??ir
                           .-ivthuhsaencrl,;?lrjuj?;;-.-?lunnnnjvu&dwofjnr.
                           .?r?nfzwkeouuozz&tcv;;;?,... ..,;;-;oegmdek&?-
                           ,?tcosssakcz??nzznllr?;-; -,.     ??;o-,.
                          ..;vfkkon&ec??in?;vrt????;;;.-     ,..;a.
                          .-cnzwkeynl?vjii?zu;;-??i;,;;?;;-...;v&u.
                           .;lnwkhgefzcz&&viivrul???;..v;     .?r;;j.
                           ..?jxx&&e&jlffovvl?lcn;t?- .c     .?-. -?
                            ,;lznkekexfwvjjc;rccoi?;. ,-    .;;.  .;
            .;t;;..,.    . .-;;tuaeeefft?ll;lr??;;;. ?.   .;?;.   ,
      -. . .,;;;. ...-;. ..-,;rzgdgyxc??????;;;;;  j. .-jr,. ,;
   .?oe;;    ,,.. ?kx?, .,.. -;?t&gbges??;v?;;?-;, ;?,.????..-;.
-??ebmazccaa?-;?zvcrui?. .-,.-;emgkuji;?;,,;-;,;l?ncecvr?t?;, .,.... . .
.-;ijvrnwl;;;jnf;;;.,;. ,;;,..;;;sdezttj?;-.,..ncjemmdbgkoz?;-.  ,-;;;.
       .-,,..  ,r??rn?;,?ojn?usxc;,omhzz?,...-?t&femqpbgddejzol;-.,-..?;?-;;-.-.
        .-,     .,-?voc;rfagdmmkeeezseeyknir?rrcrundbbkr?znoonj??.  ..         .;-..,
            .,,.-j??-.,;;,;wkeoye?layuose;vn?yj;l-?....;?n-;;sdfggi;...        -, ,...
           .,.-leer   -rzjijlr;;-?;-..;;;?i;,-.-;,;.       .,-;?, .   .
                 . ..  -...;ij- .-..;-;; .;;;;;-;l?;      ,,-;-,,.
                     .  ...,          .     .?;,-?lr; ..          .
```

blimey everything lies veiled in numbers and shapes though i can see how g turns in on itself is apt to be more self searching more analytical than c thats numerology for you finding meaning where none exists who am i to say seventh june call nick for the first time has an idea of a simple visual g related to the childs struggle to read that difficult g its all uphill from there really the alphabet the imagination and the poster design the seventh letter the magical number seven with clothes on such a spiritual number but forget it i didnt choose g g chose me hebrews romans britons gimel gamma g it appears im deeper thinking than c oh you can look for hidden meanings if you want yet when youre learning to read g is simply a little devils way of climbing up into the alphabet and beyond into your imagination at least thats what old nick says great idea the best one wins no primadonna thinking here as for me some days i feel so grrr some days i feel so gaga i think i need a drink and g stands for guinness stout not lager.

Hh

Nokia Design, Brand Team + Martin Lee

Martin's diary

6 May 2004 Receive the brief by email. I've got the letter H. Very strict instructions about the timescales: "...we can't afford to have an exhibition or a book with only 25 letters/posters." As the daunting reality of the exercise kicks in, I wonder if I can get off the hook by suggesting that H has been dropped.

9 May Found an obscure website that reckoned H to be the most boring letter of the alphabet. Hmmm. H has a pretty good riposte against this accusation: it's a high-concept letter. Think heaven, hell, hate, holocaust, H-block, H-bomb and heart.

14 May Learnt yesterday that the designer assigned to the letter H is Andrew Monk, who is head of the brand design team at Nokia. Sent him an email today.

15 May Tried to remember any time I've ever consciously thought about the letter H. Could only dredge up two occasions.

When I was at school, we had to do a maths exercise involving looking for lines of symmetry in each letter of the alphabet. H was, and I suppose still is, the only consonant that has two lines of symmetry. (OK, I'll grant you X as well, but that's got loads of other advantages.)

Second, I remember reading a novel by Rolf Hochhuth and thinking how unusual it was to have a eight-letter name starting and ending with H and with two Hs sandwiched in the middle as well. To the best of my knowledge, the only other word with similar qualities is hashish.

17 May Phoned up by Andrew. He's in a frantic spell of work but will have time to devote to the project in a few weeks. It's going to be a collaborative effort from his side as he will include his team. I can use the next couple of weeks to experiment with ideas.

18 May I wonder if there's some mileage in looking at the symbolism of the two parallel lines and the connector. Heaven and hell linked by limbo? The two lines would never meet if extended indefinitely, but the small mediating line, exactly in the middle, acts as a bridge.

I'M THE GHOST, LIKE IN 'GHOST': YOU MIGHT NOT MISS ME IF I WASN'T THERE. BARELY A BREATH. A WILL O' THE WHISPERER. I'M FOR SOPHISTICATION, ATTACHING MYSELF AS WEIGHTLESSLY AS POSSIBLE INTO WORDS. I'M A SHADOW IN THE RHYTHM OF SPOKEN LANGUAGE, BUT THERE AS PLAIN AS DAY ON THE PAGE.

20 May Interested in the combining and transforming qualities of H. The way it teams up with S, C, P, T, G, W and even R sometimes to transform letter sounds.

21 May Funny how H is at the centre of the class system. Dropping your aitches is a signal, and putting them in where they don't exist suggests you are trying too hard to be in a class where you don't belong. Thus: "I 'ave hanxieties about my aitches."

And what about this word aitch? How come other letters don't have names? Perhaps W does, but that's more a description of how it used to look than a name as such. What's the deal with aitch?

22 May If you drop the H from Hadrian's Wall, you get Adrian's Wall. Hardly the same gravitas really.

24 May H turns up in some mad places. What's the first one doing in ophthalmology? And the second one in haemorrhage for that matter? Maybe there was an H glut at some point in the past, and to use them up people dropped them into medical words hoping no one would notice.

26 May Flying back from Sydney. Finally get round to writing a couple of first drafts. It's ridiculously hard. There's everything to say and nothing. It's one thing to have ideas about H, it's quite another to get something down on paper.

Tried one pretentious effort inspired by Georges Perec's E-less novel, although I have to concede that doing without H for a couple of hundred words isn't on the same scale of achievement; it's more about getting it out of my system. Then another idea that I adopted from the illuminated religious manuscripts in the British Library, taking my cue from the look of H and the themes of heaven and hell that I thought about a couple of weeks ago.

28 May Stumble across the book we've all been exhorted to read, called *The Alphabet*. Discover that the letter H is surprisingly controversial and that some authorities don't consider it to be a letter at all. Apparently some languages would create an accent for the job that H gets up to in English.

Designers:
Visual communication and concept development by Monk/Holt/Merrick_Nokia Design, Brand Team

Writer: Martin Lee
Martin Lee keeps the wolf from the door by helping brands remain true to themselves and relevant to their customers, hopefully at the same time. This allows him to indulge his loves of family, books, football and bad puns.

30 May Getting increasingly drawn to H's status as an outsider, an impostor, a letter that doesn't belong, with no claim to legitimacy. Start a couple of efforts that explore this in fiction. One of them is embarrassingly bad – H speaking as a character in dialogue with a therapist – but I do like the idea of turning H into a personality.

2 June Do one very minimalist poster, simply on the dropping your aitches pun. Nice from a design point of view, but even for my taste it's content-lite.

20 June Finally have an idea I really like. The H in ghost feels perfect. It's there and not there, ghostly. It gets to the heart of what the letter's all about. Get a noirish sense of H as a shade, an influence rather than a presence.

1 July Eventually meet up with Andrew and Chris at Nokia in Farnborough. With eight directions in front of us, we quickly reach agreement about the ghost idea. They tactfully but correctly suggest halving the text and can see how they can use design to harmonize with the idea.

2 July Start the job of tightening up the writing and send it over.

14 July It's been nerve-wracking, but I finally get seven or eight approaches from Chris. As with the original writing, there are a couple of stand-out designs where the potential integration between text and design is immediately obvious. Talk to Chris and agree the direction to follow. It's going to happen…

Ii

Derek Birdsall + Jim Davies

For me, being paired with Derek Birdsall was a bit like finding out you're on the same team sheet as George Best. Not that Derek's one for mazy dribbles from the half-way line, you understand. Just that his work and reputation blazed before him.

He was a little elusive at first. My introductory emails seemed to disappear into a black hole hovering above north London. So, I made do with his new book, *Notes on Book Design*. It was so personal and personable that by the time we finally hooked up, I felt I already knew him.

It turns out that Derek is not much of a one for email. Or mobile phones. Or any new-fangled technology really. But he eventually phoned me, and we arranged to meet at his alma mater, Central School of Art in Holborn. It was the last week of his show there featuring (incredibly) 50 years of his graphic design work, and he promised to buy me lunch afterwards.

I arrived on the dot. Derek bustled in a little later, bearded and slightly bohemian, apologizing for his tardiness. He quickly went on to recount an anecdote about sleeping in the nearby subway the night before his interview at Central almost half a century earlier. He had travelled down from Yorkshire, and there'd been a mix-up at the hostel he'd booked. He didn't know London at all, and was determined to stay as close to the college as possible. "God knows what I looked like when I turned up next morning," he said.

Soon we'd made our way across the road (and over the subway) to Spaghetti House, where the waiters greeted Derek like a long-lost friend. I figured he might have been there before. A good project, he assured me, invariably started with a good lunch. A medium-rare steak and several glasses of wine later, we exchanged ideas. Mine consisted of several doodles in a *Simpsons* exercise book. I felt the graphic simplicity of the capital letter I might be a way of creating a dramatic mark on a poster. I imagined a simple great slab of black on a white background, like a Rothko painting. Or a sheet made up of thousands of small strokes, like so many ants crawling across the surface. Or perhaps set at an angle to look like rain.

Curiously, Derek's solution was far more word-based. He had a piece of paper folded in half with a round hole cut out of one side. You could see text through the hole, and when you opened the

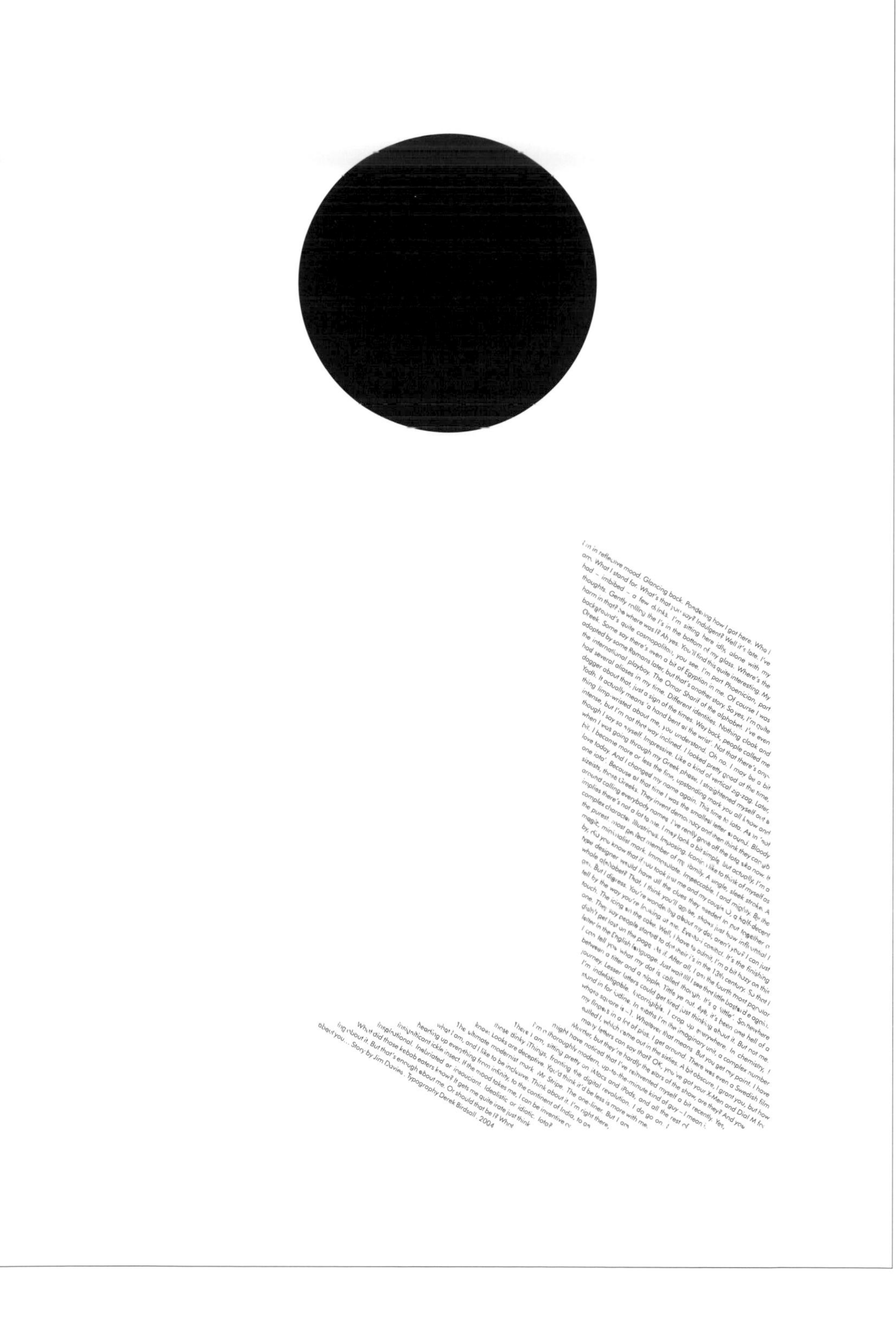
Story by Jim Davies. Typography Derek Birdsall. 2004

I'm in reflective mood. Glancing back. Pondering how I got here. Who I
am. What I stand for. What's that you say? Indulgent? Well it's late. I've
had – imbibed – a few drinks. I'm sitting here idly, alone with my
thoughts. Gently rolling the I's in the bottom of my glass. Where's the
harm in that? So where was I? Ah yes. You'll find this quite interesting. My
background's quite cosmopolitan, you see. I'm part Phoenician, part
Greek. Some say there's even a bit of Egyptian in me. Of course I was
adopted by some Romans later, but that's another story. So yes, I'm quite
the international playboy. The Omar Sharif of the alphabet. I've even
had several aliases in my time. Different identities. Nothing cloak and
dagger about that, just a sign of the times. Way back, people called me
Yodh. It actually means 'a hand bent at the wrist'. Not that there's anything limp-wristed about me, you understand. Oh no. I may be a bit
intense, but I'm not that way inclined. I looked pretty good at the time,
though I say so myself. Impressive. Like a kind of vertical zig-zag. Later,
when I was going through my Greek phase, I straightened myself out a
bit. I became more or less the fine, upstanding mark you all know and
love today. And I changed my name again. This time to Iota. As in 'not
one iota'. Because at that time I was the smallest letter around. Bloody
sizeists, those Greeks. They invent democracy and then think they can go
around calling everybody names. I've really gone off the Iota aka now. It
implies there's not a lot to me. I may look a bit simple, but actually, I'm a
complex character. Illustrious. Imposing. Iconic. I like to think of myself as
the purest, most perfect member of my family. A single, sleek stroke. A
magic, minimalist mark. Immaculate. Impeccable. I and mighty. By the
by, did you know that if you took just me and my cousin O, a half-decent
type designer would have all the clues they needed to put together a
whole alphabet? That, I think you'll agree, shows just how influential I
am. But I digress. You're wondering about my dot, aren't you? I can just
tell by the way you're looking at me. Eye-to-i contact. It's the finishing
touch. The icing on the cake. Well, I have to admit, I'm a bit hazy on this
one. They say people started to dot their i's in the 13th century. So that I
didn't get lost on the page. As if. After all, I am the fourth most popular
letter in the English language. Just wait till I see that little bastard e again.
I can tell you what my dot is called though. It's a 'tittle'. Somewhere
between a titter and a nipple. Tittle ye not. Aye, it's been one hell of a
journey. Lesser letters could get tired just thinking about it. But not me.
I'm indefatigable. Incorrigible. I crop up everywhere. In chemistry, I
stand in for iodine. In maths I'm the imaginary unit, a complex number
whose square is –1. Whatever that means. But you get my point. I have
my fingers in a lot of pies. I get around. There was even a Swedish film
called I, which came out in the sixties. A bit obscure, I grant you, but how
many letters can say that? OK, you've got your X-Men and Dial M for
Murder, but they're hardly the stars of the show, are they? And you
might have noticed that I've reinvented myself a bit recently. Yes,
I'm a thoroughly modern, up-to-the-minute kind of guy – I mean i.
There I am, sitting pretty on iMacs and iPods, and all the rest of
those dinky iThings, fronting the digital revolution. I do go on, I
know. Looks are deceptive. You'd think it'd be less is more with me.
The ultimate modernist mark. Mr Stripe. The one-liner. But I am
what I am, and I like to be inclusive. Think about it. I'm right there,
heading up everything from infinity, to the continent of India, to an
insignificant ickle insect. If the mood takes me, I can be inventive or
inspirational. Inebriated or insouciant. Idealistic or idiotic. Iota?
What did those kebab eaters know? It gets me quite irate just thinking about it. But that's enough about me. Or should that be I? What
about you… Story by Jim Davies . Typography Derek Birdsall . 2004

Designer: Derek Birdsall
Derek Birdsall's work has encompassed Penguin covers, Pirelli calendars, Monty Python, prayer books and (most recently) postage stamps. Through the process of eliminating redundancies, he works towards forms that are apparently irreducible and seemingly inevitable.

Writer: Jim Davies
Jim Davies writes for and about the design industry. As well as helping clients and communications agencies make their words work harder, he has a monthly column in *Design Week* and writes for the newspapers.

Letter: I
The letter I is alive, well and as irrepressible as ever, continuing to make its inimitable mark throughout the Western world.

paper, it revealed a dictionary definition of I, set in a neat column. The hole became the dot (or "tittle," as I later learned it was called).

We kept drinking and talking about I, and suddenly it seemed obvious that we should print the design on a reflective surface. That way, viewers would be looking at themselves as they looked at the poster. It seemed to encapsulate the narcissism of the letter, but also question the relationship of the viewer to the piece. Who's looking at whom? Just who is I? Once we'd settled on this route, it seemed to work on many different levels and open up many different possibilities.

My part of the bargain was to go away and write a short story, which Derek would then set to look like a giant I. I took nearly all my cues from the gift of a letter we'd been allocated. Clearly, it had to be written in the first person. It had to start with an I. And there had to be as many puns and outlandish words beginning with I in it as possible. It was a chance to portray an egocentric, self-obsessed character. Someone who loved bigging himself up. The big "I am."

Derek, as I discovered over lunch, is a great raconteur, and I wanted to reflect this by having I tell an amusing, slightly rambling anecdote. So it became the story of how the letter I had developed from ancient times, told in character.

I sent it to Derek, and waited. And waited. Oh my God, I thought, he hates it. On the third day he phoned. "It's great," he said. "Perfect."

Derek made one further refinement. He set the words as the shadow of an I rather than the I itself. The form of the I becomes a piece of negative space, the words seemingly cast by it. Yet more questions about identity and the reliability of the narrator are raised.

The partnership worked well. We gave each other the respect and space to do what we do best. The words and image seemed to gel organically. When I asked Derek if he wanted to write half of this diary piece, he declined politely. He said one person should do it, otherwise we'd end up sounding like Tweedledum and Tweedledee. Quite right. After all, I am I, and so is he.

Jj

Christian Altmann & Stuart Youngs + Will Awdry

Will's diary

25 May 2004 Christian and Stuart at CDT welcome me to their studio with open arms and a daunting array of work. The clarity and elegant simplicity of their design sing out. Their infectious enthusiasm is equally vocal.

Bringing J to life is our job. Up to now, we'd probably never given it a second thought. We agree to jump out of the plane together and see where we land.

Early observations swirl around us. That J is a half-formed letter without much definition or character; that the dot on the lower-case form is interesting; that J is frequently – indeed, almost exclusively – the first letter of a word.

Christian's Swiss perspective is invaluable. It is he who draws our attention to this "front door" quality. He worries away at the thought for the next fortnight, and produces an idea where the door has become a face. It's definitely a contender.

On the same theme, we discover J is the first letter of so many authoritarian, institutional and religious words: Jesus, Jerusalem, Jehovah, Judaism, Jewry, Jupiter, Juno, Janus. (We pause, design-wise, to look both ways.) Judges, justice, as well as a staunch supply of biblical stalwarts like John, James and – less reliably – Judas. Where it appears within a word, it often feels imported into English: Raj, Taj, Major...

We also confess personal connections to the letter. My mother, brother and son's names begin with J. Stuart's mother and brother too. We're not sure where this leads. Our thoughts become disconnected improvisations that in turn bring the word "jazz" into the room. Like a wombling sax, the impetus fizzles out.

4 June I am surrounded by J. The letter jumps out, underlined and in heavy bold to my way of reading and listening. My days are spent doing jury service. The judge comments on the judiciary. J-Lo hawks her behind into the tabloids again, Jordan her upper storey. In Euro 2004, new England goalkeeper David James is the subject of much pub talk. Journalists. Journals. Joy. Jack-of-all-trades. The obsession is hopelessly banal. My antennae are tuned in, the imagination yet to turn on.

Written by Will Awdry | Designed by Christian Altmann & Stuart Youngs at CDT | Made by Wood & Wood

I'm J, the latecomer here. Last to join the 26. Emerging as a murky and fumbled letter between consenting scholars during the 1500s, I was pulling my alphabetical weight by 1640. Had to wait for the 'big hello' until that 1828 monster, Webster's Dictionary. So I missed the centuries of scribbling monks, the quill thing, all the gold leaf. Never once opened the batting for a paragraph of Beowulf. Was never illuminated like my siblings. No one ever got Medieval on my (curvy) ass and thrusting upright. This is my chance to shine, my 21st Century moment. Last maybe. Least, never.

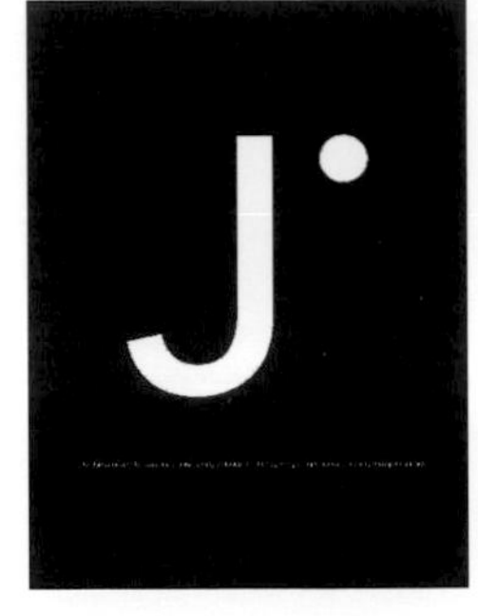

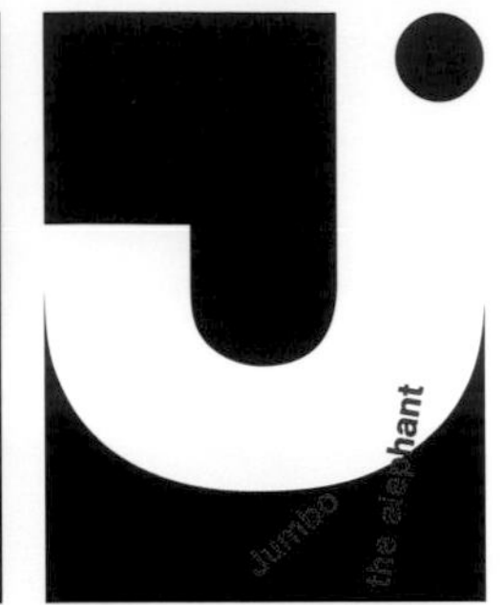

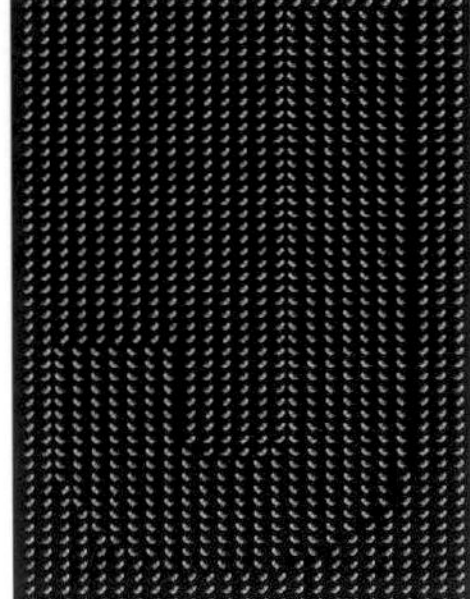

A lifelong writer friend – Jim Davies - phones me. He'd learned that J was the last to join the alphabet and seems not to have arrived (thank you David Sacks) until 1640, gaining full acceptance in *Webster's Dictionary* in 1828.

Poor thing. It missed the ecclesiastical attention of early scholars and monks. It was never hand-rendered in beautiful vermillion or garish woad. A thought strikes. It is, literally, a light-bulb moment. The thought is *illumination*.

8 June Emails between Christian, Stuart and me bat back and forth. I title one "jay-walking." The witty response is an idea of J composed entirely of jay birds.

Dismissed early from jury service in Parliament Square, I visit the British Library to join up. The experience is a cross between being granted political asylum and going to a swanky swimming pool. I marvel at my reader's card, use the lockers and creep into the Business Reading Room. The volume of stuff on J the online catalogue reveals is daunting but exciting. I retire, clinging to the light-bulb thought, anticipating many happy returns.

The brief has definitely become to render J as the twenty-first century version of a mediaeval illuminated letter.

22 June The initial designs are really promising. The chaps have finished up a gloriously sixties-inspired Jumbo the elephant idea, but the illuminated neon is the favourite by consensus. Any fears that we'd end up with Malibu-style Coconut Grove pink neon evaporate; Christian and Stuart's take on it is clean and contemporary.

Over the next few days, I have to write the copy. Christian and Stuart have enlisted the help of Wood & Wood to help make the poster as an actual 3D working sign, and John Ross to photograph it. Their contributions are invaluable.

29 June I prevaricate, procrastinate, sharpen every pencil available in a bid to avoid writing the copy, but eventually send over a piece. Two or three days of tact from the team help hone and kern it to their satisfaction.

Designer: Christian Altmann
A graduate of Basel's Safe Haven Typography, Christian left Switzerland in 1996, travelling via Munich and New York to London's CDT in 2000. It's now his home, where he thinks in a Swiss-German-American-English kind of way...

Designer: Stuart Youngs
A 1996 Bath graduate, Stuart tapped into typography at Mytton Williams before moving to CDT, where he is now a creative associate. His designs have covered a waterfront from Royal Mail to the London Chamber Orchestra.

Writer: Will Awdry
An advertising copywriter turned creative director, Will has spent most of his career at Bartle Bogle Hegarty and is now at DDB London. He dreams, one day, of writing more than 100 words.

We have created a brilliantly shiny character looking for love, if not pleading for charity. Plaintive, petulant, arriviste and of ambivalent gender, it's still a bit sexy, a bit "bling bling." Its voice has an adolescent complexity.

As for creative tension between the co-creators of J, I have to report that we haven't been a *Big Brother* house. No spats at all. I wish my other job were as much fun.

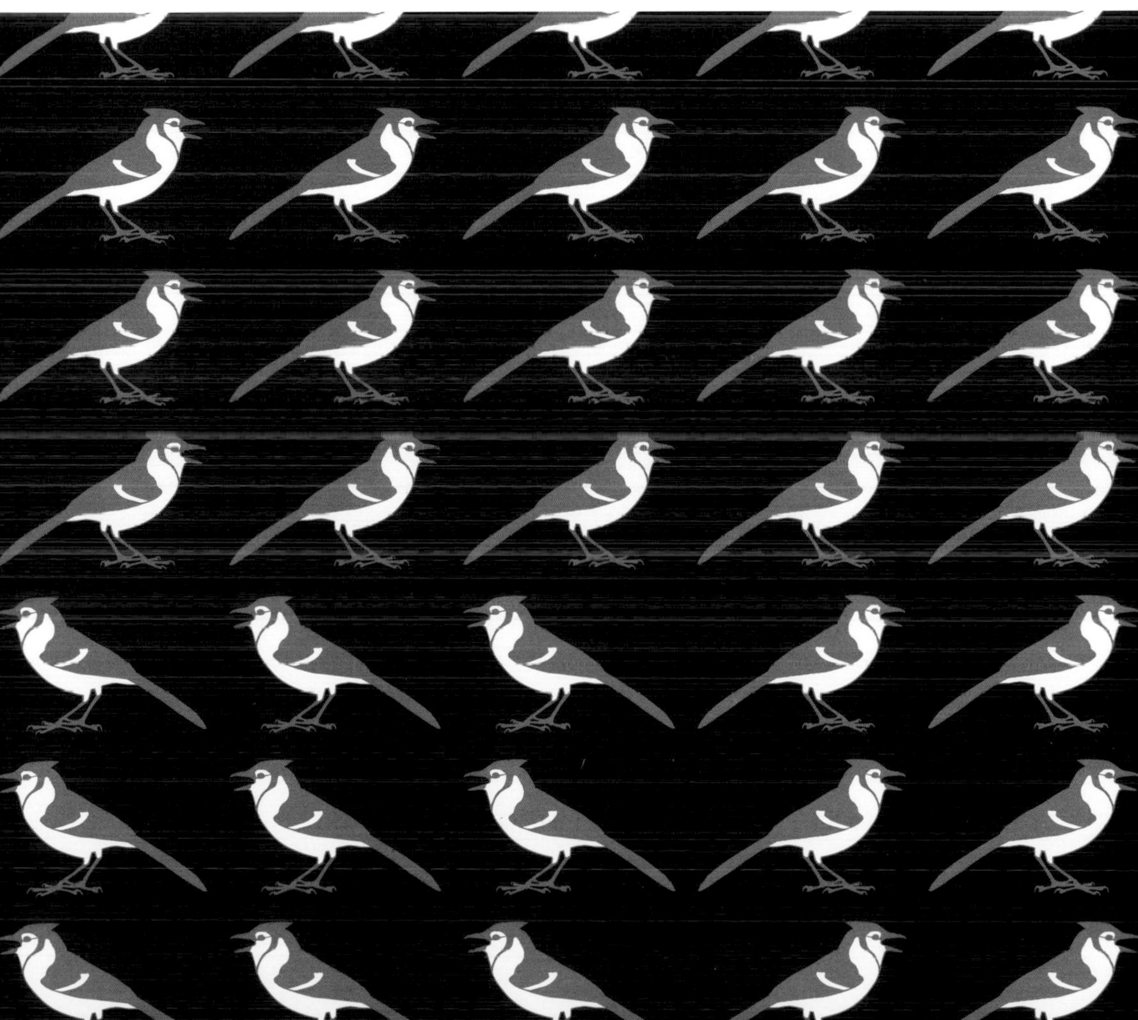

Marksteen Adamson + Neil Taylor

Neil's diary

Typical. A list of famous, revered, extraordinary designers, and I get the one I used to work with. Not that Marksteen isn't also famous, or revered, and he's certainly extraordinary. But when I saw the list of collaborators, and spotted his name next to my letter, here's what I thought:

1. It's Marksteen. He's going to be a nightmare to get to meetings.
2. It's Marksteen. He's going to have 400 ideas every minute, and we'll never agree on one.
3. Even if we can agree, when we go away and do our bits they'll mutate and never fit together.
4. He's a designer. He'll supply the final artwork with the words I've agonized over misspelt. I'll look daft in front of the famous, revered, extraordinary writers who've also got letters to write about.

Oh well, better the devil you know. In the end, only bits of my worries turned out to be true. And some of them were completely wrong. Marksteen's even been chasing me about meetings (what *is* going on? Moving to the Thames Valley has obviously left him a changed man).

We had our first meeting at the British Library, outside, in the sun, surrounded by bookish researchers dazzled by their first bit of natural light all day. I was quite nervous (see point 2). But as it happened, we'd both been thinking about similar things.

The British Library's all about preservation, so Marksteen, being a contrary type of character, wanted to make a poster that was about the opposite. And he didn't just want a poster that couldn't be preserved; he wanted one that was edible.

And so far, the writers' group 26 has been all about English, so as a recovering linguistics geek (and also a slightly contrary type of character), I wanted to write about other languages. Particularly, I'd been thinking about the half of the world's languages being squashed out of life by the others. Languages that are running out of speakers. Or rather, their speakers are running out on them, and into the arms of the powerful, popular ones like English.

Our plan was starting to come together. Decay. Extinction. A barrel of laughs.

KACHAHLHLICHI

[kachahl-li-chi]

EAT MY WORDS

The British Library exists to preserve words. But of around 6,000 languages in the world, a half are under threat. Think of the outcry if half the world's population was dying, and only the powerful or popular survived. That's what's happening to these languages.

If these languages do dwindle and die, we will be able to preserve the words, but not their spirit. Words like ki', an Earth spirit in Taino, from the Bahamas. Ka'nikonriio: beauty, law, or goodness in Mohawk. Or ketawyapyeske, a ring around the moon in Potawatomi, from the Great Lakes of the North America.

We can try to translate them, but we'll never fully understand the way of life, or the way of thinking, that brought them about. Culture and language are married. That's why Welsh culture is flourishing as its language steps back from the brink of extinction.

Like some of these 'k' words, this poster won't survive either. It is designed to disappear. Even if the Library wanted to preserve it, the materials will deteriorate, and vanish.

Words will only live if people choose to use them, to make them part of themselves. So this poster is edible. These are words you really can eat.

Oh, and in the threatened native language of Alabama. 'KACHAHLHLICHI' means 'to let someone have a bite'.

100% edible

Best before 01.01.05

Eating instructions

Peel poster away from backing

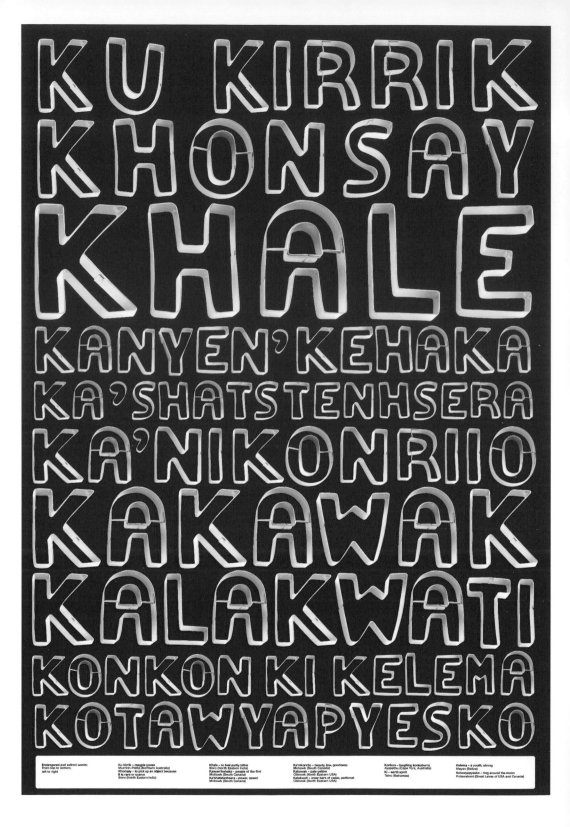

KU KIRRIK
KHONSAY
KHALE
KANYEN'KEHAKA
KA'SHATSTENHSERA
KA'NIKONRIIO
KAKAWAK
KALAKWATI
KONKON KI KELEMA
KOTAWYAPYESKO

Endangered and extinct words:
From top to bottom,
left to right

Ku kirrik – magpie goose
Murrinh-Patha (Northern Australia)
Khonsay – to pick up an object because it is rare or scarce
Boro (North Eastern India)

Khale – to feel partly bitter
Boro (North Eastern India)
Kanyen'kehaka – people of the flint
Mohawk (South Canada)
Ka'shatstenhsera – power, speed
Mohawk (South Canada)

Ka'nikonriio – beauty, law, goodness
Mohawk (South Canada)
Kakawak – pale yellow
Chinook (North Eastern USA)
Kalakwati – inner bark of cedar, petticoat
Chinook (North Eastern USA)

Konkon – laughing kookaburra
Ayapathu (Cape York, Australia)
Ki – earth spirit
Taino (Bahamas)

Kelema – a youth, strong
Mayan (Belize)
Kotawyapyesko – ring around the moon
Potawatomi (Great Lakes of USA and Canada)

Designer: Marksteen Adamson
Marksteen is founder and creative director of ArthurSteenAdamson. A fifteen-year career in branding has left him remarkably young-looking. And he's worked with brands like Orange, countries like Estonia, and even a church in Cornwall.

Writer: Neil Taylor
I'm a writer and trainer at The Writer. A Lancastrian exiled to London, and a *québécois* French speaker, I know language is a big part of our identity. So I help people think about that.

Next, I collected lovely words from dying languages that start with a K (or at least the sound we write in our alphabet with a K; lots of these languages have never been written down). Words like *ki'*, "earth spirit" in Taino, from the Bahamas. *Ka'nikonriio*: "beauty, law or goodness" in Mohawk. Or *kotawyapyesko*, "ring around the moon" in Potawatomi, from the Great Lakes of North America. And, of course, the word that has pride of place on our poster: *kachahlhlchi*, which means "to let someone have a bite" in the threatened native language of Alabama. Here's a tip: pronounce "hl" like "ll" in Welsh and it's easier to say. We can try to preserve these words, and to translate them, but we'll never fully understand the way of life, or the way of thinking, that brought them about. Culture and language are married. Read *Spoken Here* by Mark Abley to see some of the ones we didn't have room for. We both had a soft spot for the Indian word that means "to feel *partly* bitter."

So. An edible poster, and some dying words. Words you really could eat. I liked the idea that the only way to keep these dying languages alive is if they're part of people's culture and identity – if people make them part of themselves. We're hoping that it'll be the world's biggest-ever edible poster (OK, there's not much competition). It'll taste of white chocolate. Marksteen even created a unique typeface for it, made from photos of cookie cutters. And after the exhibition people can have a bite – we're going to cut up our poster into little bits for people to buy and eat.

Suddenly things seemed a little bit cheerier. Now there was only point 3 to worry about (but luckily Marksteen's been working with his colleague Scott on the layout, who's been keeping him on the straight and narrow). In fact, it's all been worryingly painless… so far. We're still talking. There were lots of different threads of inspiration, but put it all together and it seemed to make some kind of sense. To us, at least; you can decide when you see it. And as I write this, I've still got one set of fingers crossed on point 4.

Tom Green + Mary Whenman

Mary's diary

May 2003 I'm driving through Torquay with my friend Margaret Oscar. She tells me about a writing group she's involved in called 26. I immediately see the group's relevance to my work in public relations.

September 2003 Launch of 26. I send off my membership cheque and I'm assigned a letter. I wanted M for Mary but it had gone. I take L for no other reason than it's next to M in the alphabet – clearly a well-considered decision. I think no more of it.

20 April 2004 An email from John Simmons and a phone call from Margaret with details of the 26 and ISTD poster project. I've never been asked to participate in anything like this before. Exciting. Overwhelming too. I think no more of it.

6 May I receive the poster brief. All I can think is "What have I got myself into?" My managing director has just resigned and I'm the only board director in the agency. Two members of my team leave and my associate director is seconded to a client for three days a week. I start working 14-hour days just to keep afloat. I see my husband only at weekends. I file the poster brief. I think no more of it.

13 May I receive the name of my poster design partner. He lives in Australia.

24 May I send an email to my designer. He replies and we schedule a time to speak in a few days.

2 June We still haven't spoken. I email again and write "I'd like to keep it minimal (I hope you do minimal) along the lines of love, life, laughter."

The designer calls. He says the project should be collaborative and wants to contribute to the writing of the poster as well as the design. He doesn't like my words. He says he'll go away and think further.

I never hear from him again.

29 June Margaret emails to ask if there are any special requirements for my poster. Yes – a designer.

Love
Life
Laughter

Designer: Tom Green
Tom Green graduated from Kingston University in 2001 with a first-class honours degree. He has worked as a designer for Grade Design for three years and collaborated on the design of the ISTD website.

Writer: Mary Whenman
Mary Whenman has been a corporate public relations consultant for 14 years, advising companies at point of change on reputation management. She has worked for clients including Orange, De Beers, Butlins and Cadbury Schweppes.

A rapid round of texts and emails begins between Margaret and me while she's on holiday in Cornwall. I need a new designer, preferably someone in London who can work fast.

8 July My knight arrives in the form of Peter Dawson, chair of the publications committee for ISTD. He says he will take care of everything. He assigns Tom Green, one of the designers from his agency, to work with me. I email Tom. He replies, saying "Love the words!"

13 July We meet. Tom has worked over the weekend to develop ideas, sourcing material from the British Library. We discuss a number of creative approaches and agree on a sixties retro-psychedelic look. I leave feeling excited and lucky to be involved in the project.

Tom's diary

It's 8 July and Mary's designer partner has dropped out. I am asked to step into his shoes. With a certain amount of trepidation, I agree and am given a small ream of briefs and a deadline of three weeks. A poster in three weeks? No problem.

Love, life, laughter. The colour red is lodged in my head and so too the image of a heart. Not the cartoon icon but an accurate scientific illustration. I plunder the British Library for anatomical drawings the following day, revelling in museum catalogues of Leonardo's drawings and dissection guides for medical students. It's not working, though. I'm trying to illustrate words that are essentially warm and playful with images that are cold and scientific.

Positive, passionate, life-affirming, uplifting. Mary's words call out for a design that radiates warmth. I find a poster by Michael English for the 1967 Love Festival, all swirly type and glossy cartoon lips. This is more like it. An old Jackson Five 45 in its EMI sleeve, a mass of psychedelic rings and discs. The inside collar of a new Vicri shirt with bright pink interweaving petals. Inspired, I sketch stripes, spots, flowers, bubbles, colours, patterns and textures, all interacting with the type.

I meet Mary for the first time on 13 July and find we're both agreed (and enthusiastic) about the look of the poster. I've got the green light and can't wait to start.

Mm

Angus Hyland + Sarah McCartney

Sarah's diary

Apparently I arrived in this world two weeks early, but I have spent much of my life being late.

I missed the coffee and networking at the British Library session but arrived in time to be mesmerized, fascinated and slightly depressed by curator Michelle Brown's knowledge and love of ancient manuscripts. (Depressed only because I wish I knew that much about anything at all.) Getting my temporary British Library reader's pass and discovering that "temporary" meant three years almost made me cry (in a good way). I left via the bookshop with many books on letters.

M had been my letter since I joined 26. It is M for McCartney; it is right in the middle of things; and it is Judi Dench in the Bond films.

I had emailed Angus Hyland about meeting at the event, but he didn't turn up. He called me later. He hadn't wanted M, he told me; he wanted an asymmetrical letter. He didn't really like the design of the British Library. He wasn't a typographer either. I was thinking, I said, about the mathematical significance of M. That was not at all the way he'd been thinking about it.

Just as I was about to resign as M, Angus invited me to Pentagram for coffee and cakes and gave me a helpful detailed description of where his offices hide themselves in West London. I also looked up their website and packed my A–Z just in case. I allowed loads of time to get there, determined not to be late for my first encounter with the fabled five-pointed temple to fine design, but blew it stuck on the Central Line at White City.

It's worth visiting Pentagram to meet the lovely man who runs reception and to see the exhibition there. (The one I saw, showing art in ballpoint pen, was curated by Angus.) Round the corner, across the courtyard, inside the former dairy building, I sat on black leather in an atrium, surrounded by old brick, new glass, smooth pebbles and cold steel. Angus escorted me into a glass meeting room and showed me the latest Pentagram book. It fell open naturally at an essay on his work. I countered with a copy of the *Lush Times* and two Bath Ballistics. Light dawned: I was to be working with a design god. As ever, my mouth worked faster than my brain.

"You forgot the cake then?" I said, and spent the rest of the meeting kicking myself.

LIKE LIFE, CAME FROM THE SEA

R, "MEM", WITH THE UNEVEN, UNDULATING SHAPE MADE BY WAVES ON THE
E ROMANS TIDIED IT UP INTO FOUR STRAIGHT LINES WHICH WAS JUST TYPI
R BY ITS MUM AND DAD. THE MEDIEVAL, ROUNDED FORM OF M SIGNIFIES M
D TWO BROWS. THE MODERN, MYSTIC HEBREW LETTER "MEM" SIGNIFIES W

Designer: Angus Hyland
Angus Hyland joined the Pentagram London office as a partner in 1998, where he continues to work with a wide range of private- and public-sector clients. He is currently UK president of the Alliance Graphique Internationale.

Writer: Sarah McCartney
I write mostly for Lush Cosmetics. My background is maths, marketing and music. Eventually, I'd like to buy a building and turn it into a yoga centre, writing space, coffee shop and shoe museum.

We talked about M as the shape of waves on the sea, of sound waves and of mountains. As Angus was about to become a father, we talked about babies forming their first word with the sound M and whether their mothers had assumed, in a grand act of post-rationalization, that the sound "Ma" referred to themselves.

We agreed that I would write about M and send the words to Angus before he left with his wife for one last holiday on their own (without buckets and spades, factor 50 sun block, swimming floats and permanent mixed feelings of joy and anxiety). I volunteered to write this diary piece too, as Angus wasn't keen on committing to 500 words. (Try to stop me.) He'd written the introduction to the catalogue that goes with his exhibition "Ballpoint." He gave me a copy, which more than made up for the cake, and I read it on the way home. My favourite line from it is:

"Considering the omnipresence of the ballpoint pen, it seems odd that its use has been restricted to writing."

Great. My design partner could also write.

Reading my notes a couple of weeks later, I realized that Angus had long since departed for sunny shores and I had missed the first of my deadlines. I called John Simmons. "How much did you write?" I asked. "Four sentences," he replied. That reassured me a little but I had yet to find time amid *Lush Times* meetings and deadlines to visit the British Library, apart from calling at the restaurant on the way to see Ricky Gervais's one-man show at the Bloomsbury Theatre.

I had written pages of notes, waffle, thoughts, ideas and doodles on M. I had to round them up, cut them down and make some sense, then have the courage to send them to Angus.

I read my books about letters. I put "mem," "M" and "alphabet" into Google and found all kinds of interesting things; some helped, most distracted. What had I learnt? Not enough, I felt. I was still promising myself a trip to the British Library. Despite the staff's welcoming support I'd still not made it past the public areas into the hallowed halls.

I sent my M to Angus while he was still on holiday, telling him to cut anything he didn't like, which I thought was pretty reasonable and partly made up for failing miserably to supply it on time. For five days I held my breath, metaphorically speaking. The day Angus got back into the office, the following words arrived:

LIKE LIFE, CAME FROM THE SEA

M CAME INTO EXISTENCE WHEN SEA-GOING PHOENICIANS MATCHED THEIR WORD FOR WATER, "MEM", WITH THE UNEVEN, UNDULATING SHAPE MADE BY WAVES ON THE MEDITERRANEAN. (AS FAR AS WE KNOW.) BY THE TIME THE SEMITIC ALPHABET EVOLVED, M HAD ACQUIRED DEFINED, JAGGED POINTS – WITH AT LEAST ONE MORE THAN IT HAS NOW. THE ROMANS TIDIED IT UP INTO FOUR STRAIGHT LINES WHICH WAS JUST TYPICAL OF THE ROMANS. SOMETIMES THE CENTRAL POINT REACHES THE GROUND; SOMETIMES IT DANGLES BETWEEN THE TWO LATERAL SUPPORTS LIKE A CHILD SWUNG THROUGH THE AIR BY ITS MUM AND DAD. THE MEDIEVAL, ROUNDED FORM OF M SIGNIFIES MAN. GOD WAS SAID TO HAVE WRITTEN THE NAME OF MAN 'OMO' ON HIS FOREHEAD (IN LATIN, NATURALLY). THE TWO EYES WERE THE "O"S AND THE "M" TRACED THE SHAPE OF HIS NOSE AND TWO BROWS. THE MODERN, MYSTIC HEBREW LETTER "MEM" SIGNIFIES WOMAN. SO M, THE SHAPE OF THE SEA, IS THE SYMBOL OF MAN AND THE SYMBOL OF WOMEN.

"The text is perfect for inspiring a visual response. Let's leave it complete. It will take me a week or two to come up with a suitable design."

If I'd been American and not from Redcar, I might have punched the air and yelled "Woohoo!" Instead I awarded myself a bar of organic dark chocolate with cherries in it.

The deadline for this diary piece is 13 days before the deadline for the artwork. I'm trying not to look forward to seeing Angus's work too much, but I have this feeling that no matter how wonderful I already think it's going to be, it will be even better. I've never been a pessimist.

Nn

Gilmar Wendt + John Simmons

John's diary

We decided, Gilmar and I, that I would write the diary piece. Perhaps it's the obvious division of labour, as I can write the diary while Gilmar is busy designing the poster.

We met for the first time at the British Library briefing session. That was an inspiring morning, particularly the talk by Michelle Brown, curator of illuminated manuscripts. After the briefing we arranged to meet the following week but to email each other in the meantime.

Having asked for the last letter to be chosen, to gain the runt of the letters, I was intrigued that it was N. Why did people shy away from N? I felt a certain serendipitous attraction to it because it happens to be the middle initial of my name. For Gilmar it had no immediate positive attractions whatsoever.

Indeed it seemed to me to have a lot of the negative about it. No, nay, never, nothing. Non, niet, nein, nada. N is negative in all the European languages, it's how we say NO. But it stands next to O in the alphabet and, if you reverse the alphabetical order, you come up with ON. There was something appealing in the idea of turning a negative into a positive.

So I wrote a poem. I called the poem "o no n" and it became a plea for N to have its own place in the world, for us all to feel less negative about it.

When we met at the Royal Society of Arts a week later, Gilmar had read my poem. We talked about it and agreed that there was something interesting in the idea of a positive campaign for N. How can you transform a cold word into a warm one by the addition of this letter? *Ice is nice*, for example. We wondered about a campaign – *Just say ON* – for the liberation of N from negativity. Could this be N-day? Perhaps we could draw attention to N's precise virtues by pointing out what happens in its absence. *Ever say ever*. From *any* to *ay*. To prove that *something will come of nothing*.

We went our separate ways again, keeping in touch by email. Gilmar put to me three reasons for a poster. First, to make an announcement. Second, to sell. Third, to make a polemical point. The third point fitted with the idea of a campaign. He also wrote: "What does the letter mean to me? Well, it's interesting that you said this was the letter that no one wanted. N means nothing to me.

no
no
N came in one night
blown on the wind
through the window,
probably sometime soon
after I was born.
With no n
we can neither scorn
nor score points.
We lose the chance
to entrance or entertain.
N is an ingredient
in everyone's living room,
morning, noon and night.
Without n
life is so empty,
there is a positive
lack of life.
onon

Designer: Gilmar Wendt
Gilmar Wendt is creative director of SAS, London. He loves to design books and is co-author of *Schriften erkennen*, a book about the classification of typefaces that has been widely used in typographic education in Germany.

Writer: John Simmons
John Simmons is a writer, trainer and consultant. His books explore the power of creative writing and story-telling in business. He works with all kinds of people and brands to help them develop through writing.

Nobody wants to work with N. I hate it when people use a hyphen instead of an en dash."

I loved that last phrase of typographical exasperation. It related to a thought I'd had about subverting the prohibitive orthodoxy that you see around institutions. I imagined a NO ENTRY sign from which the N was removed to create OETRY: the addition of a P transformed the negativity of access denied into imagination liberated through poetry. Perhaps, then, a poem was the right response. I added to Gilmar's list of three uses for a poster the thought that, like the title of David Stuart and Beryl McAlhone's book, a poster can simply create a "smile in the mind."

Weeks passed. We arranged to meet at the British Library. I made a couple of visits during that time. The Paolozzi statue in the piazza interested me. It's a forbidding monumental sculpture based on a William Blake engraving of Newton. Like the exterior of the library itself, it looks intimidating. It has signs warning people not to climb on it, in effect another NO ENTRY sign.

I decided to research Newton and Blake. First I remembered that the newton was also a measurement in physics, and I discovered that the newton (symbol N) is a unit of force. Going further I found that Newton's third law of motion states: "When a body A exerts a force on a body B, B exerts an equal and opposite force on A; that is, to every action there is an equal and opposite reaction." Positive becomes negative, negative positive: two equal forces both contained in N.

Blake, though, was no admirer of Newton. He would have seen himself (the poet) in opposition to Newton (the scientist). The creative imagination against scientific empiricism. His engraving, Paolozzi's statue, show Newton poring over measurements, intent on detail to discover the secrets of the universe – while ignoring the beauty of the universe all around him.

The challenge for the British Library is to provide both, the negative and the positive reactions. To allow scientists and students of all kinds to pursue detailed knowledge. And to enable us all to illuminate understanding through knowledge and imagination, by seeing the big picture too, through poetry and the generation of ideas.

Meeting up with Gilmar, moving on to a long discussion over a drink, we talked about various possibilities. Gilmar had explored ideas

N came in one night
blown on the wind
through the window,
probably sometime soon
after I was born.

With no n
we can neither scorn
nor score points.
We lose the chance
to entrance or entertain.

N is an ingredient
in everyone's living room,
morning, noon and night.

Without n
life is so empty,
there is a positive
lack of life.

onon

to do with N for north, for Napoleon, for new and news, but had come back again to N for anti, the exploration of the negative. He was interested in neon colours (a short step from non). There were surprisingly few typefaces beginning with N, among them Napoleon, Neuzeit, News Gothic and Novarese.

The other ideas ranged from simple (the graffitied NO ENTRY) to multi-layered (Paolozzi's Newton, plus facsimile manuscript of Newton's law, with compasses and poem). In the end, though, Gilmar felt that my poem about N had typographic possibilities and that it had changed his initially negative response to N into a much more humane, warm approach. Showing me classic European posters from the twenties and thirties, he wanted to take the poem and create something in that typographic spirit. The screen-printed result you can see here, but it's simply the final crafted tip of the iceberg, the one that emerged from Gilmar's rigorous process of sketches, composition and exploration of type, layout and colour before printing.

Oo

Rick Sellars + Tim Rich

Notes and sketches. O. O. O. What does O represent? Circle. World. Whole. Hole. Mouth. *Ouroboros*: the serpent swallowing its tail. Cycle of nature. Fertility. Energy. So, small themes then. Just life, the universe and everything.

Flash of Mathias in Alain Robbe-Grillet's book *The Voyeur*, tracing a double circuit around the island. Characters walking in circles?

Drifting through the British Library. Man with half-moon glasses gurning behind a dictionary of folklore. Teenagers pointing at sea creatures in a manuscript map. Palimpsests; stories on stories, textual archaeology. Rush of laughter from the lecture hall. Authorial innuendo in the marginalia of missals. A nod and a wink; layers of meaning. Woman in Humanities 1 smiles discreetly as she ever so slowly turns a page.

Stuck. So many themes. Stuck. Walk in the park. Stuck. Sleep on it. Wake with a simple story fresh in my head. Scrawl it out longhand. Feels right. But hadn't expected my narrator to be a literate dog.

Edit, edit, edit. Want to weave in sly connections, ambiguities, layers. And some mouth-watering O words.

Designer partners announced. Don't know Rick. Make some calls. Highly regarded. I'm feeling bad. Usually collaborate from initial ideas to final draft. Now I'm arriving with a finished piece. What if he hates it? What if he sets it in 4 point type, white on white? What if he uses Dingbats in revenge?

Meet. A swift evening walk to a Bermondsey pub. What ifs are making me anxious. Rick is warm and thoughtful. Talk around life, design and words. He wonders how long I need to write something for the poster. I pull a draft from my bag and ghost away to the bar. Return with pints and apologies. Say I'd be happy to put this approach to one side and develop another route (a lie). No need, he says, and reads it again.

Design. Rick can easily create something elegant, but we both want to push harder than that. He emails some wonderful observations and visual ideas. He is inside the story. He's also keen to start the piece in the middle to emphasize circularity. I'm worried about confusing the reader. The circular narrative is important, but the story needs to open at the entrance to the park. That's why I start with "And" and roll the action from there. I'm fighting an urge to control the telling.

here we are again. Walking through the white gate. Then our ritual halt. Decades of back legs lifting, each story layering upon the last. A pee palimpsest. A fluid corporate identity. Done. Onward. Gathering pace. And Paradise now unfolds before me. Southwich Recreation Ground. Rodney's idea of unbridled Nature. Oh, Eden. All the characters are here, trudging their circuit. Sad orbits. I'm with William James when he wrote: 'Most people live, whether physically, intellectually or morally, in a very restricted circle of their potential being'. I'm so sorry, you didn't realise. Yes, we can read. It's really our big little secret. Keep it to yourself, please. Your kind will only patronise us; start leaving The Alchemist or old Daily Mails in our basket, or depositing scribbled recommendations next to our bowl of water each morning ('You will simply adore Bulgakov'). Despite being an idiot, Rodney does read The Observer. A rare flash of taste on his part. Uses it for my bedding. Rubbish Business section, but I like Travel and Tim Atkins' oenologisms. Look at those mutts, slaves on a leather-tether'd odyssey under a slow sun. They think the planets rotate around their owner's hand. Come on Roddy dear, stop worrying about that memo from Human Resources and unleash me. I tell you, I've come round to thinking that the world contains just two orders of creature. There are the types who treat everything as a journey from A to B—always in pursuit of the better this, the improved that. So terribly linear. Like living under a death sentence. And then there are those who enjoy the bliss of now. The pure joy of chasing one's tail to the point of hilarious, delicious, satisfying exhaustion. An end in itself. A sexy, earnest German Shepherd once told me "There is no omphalos out there waiting to be discovered. We create it ourselves." We create it ourselves. Ouroboros. Right, let me off this bloody lead, Rodders, you dullard. My years are shorter than yours. I have things to do. I have footballs to puncture and rubber rings to chomp. Floating Frisbees to head-butt and looping kites to intercept. Stacking planes to whine at and great rolling clouds to fall in love with—head over heels over head over heels in love. Let me go. I have a million ideas to dance before I lay down and let my circle draw itself to a stop. And

Designer: Rick Sellars
Rick Sellars is a graphic designer. He studied at the London College of Printing, gaining a HND and MA in typographic design. He worked for a short time in Amsterdam for Samenwerkende Ontwerpers and now works for North Design in London.

Writer: Tim Rich
Tim is a writer and editor. He works closely with designers to help large companies become eloquent. He was previously editor of *Graphics International* and a columnist for *Design Week*.

Choosing a face. Rick's found a new font by David Quay. I imagined we'd use rounded characters, but this is made from vertical lines. Can't see how it will work, but Rick has a glimmer in his eyes. And there is something interesting in the apparent conflict between a circular character and a straight face. I trust his instinct.
Play. Talk about emphasizing certain words and phrases by adding weight to the vertical strokes. On reflection, Rick feels these accents are too directional, as if we're telling the reader what to think. Suggests a subtler approach where the typographic colour emerges as the story unfolds. And if we stop and start the narrative in the middle, and run the text to the edges, the reader gets a sense of an infinitely repeating cycle. Getting there...
Final session. Rick's introduced new layers of circularity using imagery and varnish. John Ross has allowed us to incorporate one of his gorgeous sky photographs. Spencer Wallace at Nirvana Print is helping us to transform artwork into finished piece. Legibility and readability are still issues though, and we'll have to watch how well the lines of ink and varnish communicate characters and words. Still concerned that the narrative is getting lost, and we revert to the original opening, but with "and" at the end and "here" at the beginning. A story swallowing its tale.
Context. Convinced that lots of other teams will be tempted into using startling materials and formats. Giant banners made from Fair Trade hessian. Three-dimensional word sculptures serenaded by wind chimes. A luminous macramé letter suspended from the ceiling. Decide to keep it simple. Poster. Beautifully printed. Best position we can grab.
Finished work. I love the subtlety of Rick's design. It forms narrative circles using vertical lines, and draws out ideas and connections. It's been a long journey from first draft to British Library. Production creates distance between the teller and the tale. Reading the story again, I realize it's a memo to myself: Stop chasing the future and enjoy life now.

itual halt. Decades of backlogs lik
upon the last. A pee palimpsest. A R
Done. Onward. Gathering pace. And h
ne. Southwich Recreation Ground. A
Nature. Oh, Eden. All the characters
circuit. Sad orbits. I'm with William J
'Most people live, whether physically
in a very restricted circle of their po
you didn't realise. Yes, we can read.
secret. Keep it to yourself, please.
us; start leaving The Alchemist or o
or depositing scribbled recommenda
water each morning ('You will simply
being an idiot, Rodney does read Th
of taste on his part. Uses it for my
section, but I like Travel and Tim A
those mules, slaves on a leather-b
sun. They think the planets rotate
Come on Roddy dear, stop worrying
Resources and unleash me. I tell yo
that the world contains just two

Pp

Bryan Edmondson + Robert Williams

When the very long-haired man and his very short-haired friend first met at my humble Spanish bar in Belsize Park, it was obvious to me that they were on a date. A blind date even; certainly both were visibly anxious. I decided there and then to keep my eye on them, as in my extensive experience, extreme haircuts often result in excessive drinking and the non-payment of bar bills. It was also clear to me from the beginning that the pair were planning something. This is what I wrote in my notebook:

They are northern. Neither of them speaks properly. I ask their waitress what they talk about and she says: "Football, mostly. And tapas. And P."

P? Two strangers from the north of England meet up on a Friday night to hold a conversation about not even the whole alphabet? I suspect they are talking in code. Will investigate…

There are indeed notes and drawings on dog-eared emails all over their table. There are pictures of parking signs and words scrawled large in scruffy handwriting. "Paper." "Printing." "Penguin." A zoo heist? Perhaps. Certainly there is some concern from the long-hair that whatever they are planning doesn't look like an advertisement for flightless seabirds. You can see his point.

I am intrigued and decide to smoke a cigarette at the table next to them. There I discover that the long-hair is in fact referring not to the penguin of the animal kingdom, but the Penguin of the publishing world. The story of the birth of the Penguin paperback – and the fact that it is 70 years old in 2005 – seems to get the short-hair very excited. Apparently, a man named Allen Lane had the idea at Exeter railway station in 1935. He'd spent the weekend with a woman named Agatha Christie and couldn't find anything worth reading for his journey back to London. So he decided to do something about it. Lane invented the Penguin paperback that day. In so doing, he made quality writing available to the masses for the first time – oh, and changed the world for ever. Fascinating. I left.

Next time they came there were many sheets of paper split into thirds. One showed a huge book cover made up of many smaller ones. Another was partly made up of orange words – the Bible, the *Sun*, Magna Carta, *Pride and Prejudice, The Origin of Species, White Teeth* – with in the middle the title *What price printed paper?* by an

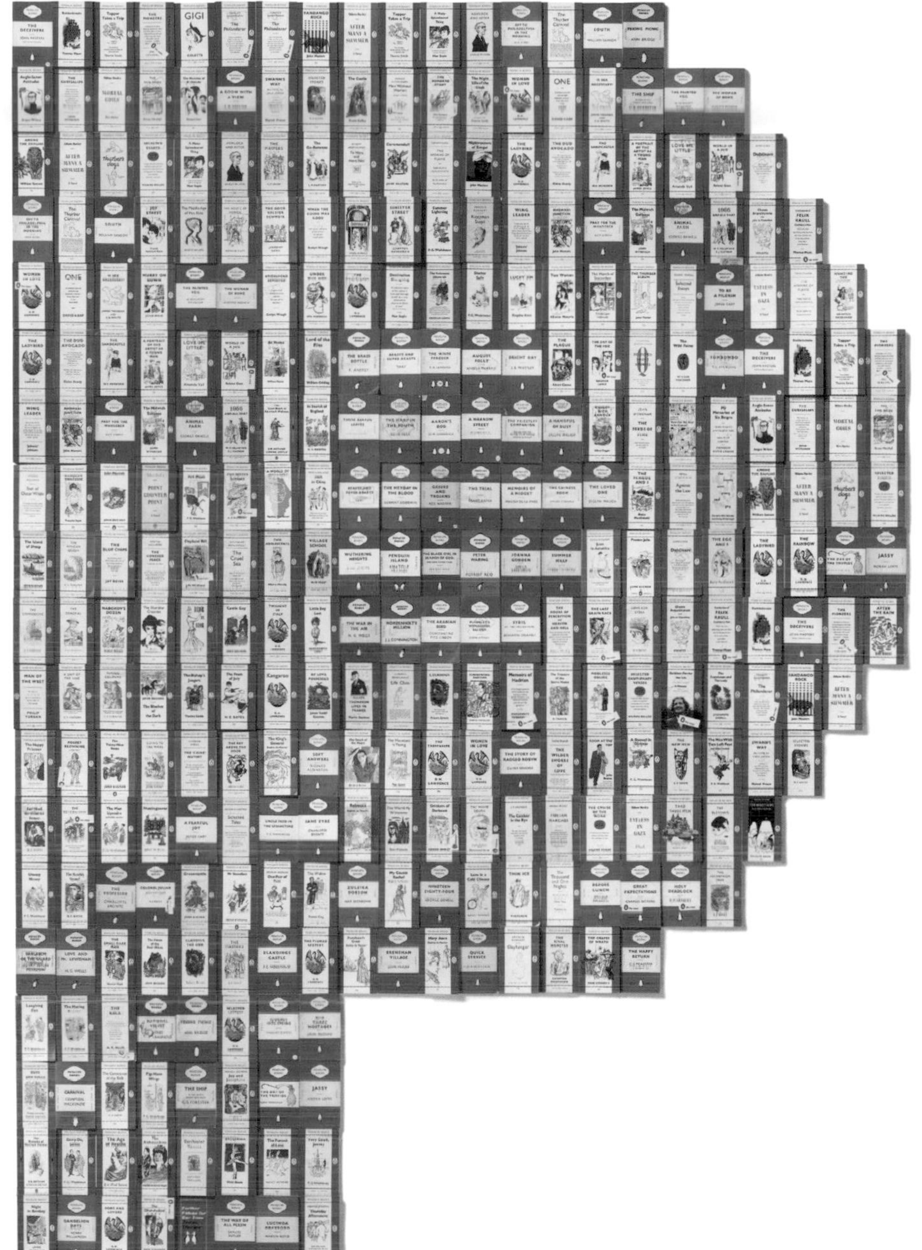

Property of the Public

26 Letters/Bryan Edmondson/Robert Williams
With thanks to Stuart Bailey/John Ross/Sue Osborne/Penguin Books
Printed by Augustus Martin with thanks to David Proud

Designer: Bryan Edmondson
Bryan Edmondson set up SEA with John Simpson in 1997. He has worked with a mix of clients including D&AD, Boots, Jigsaw, EMI, Tate, GF Smith, BBC, Matthew Williamson, furniture makers Keen and Beyon.

Writer: Robert Williams
As creative director of Penguin UK, my days invariably involve trying to engage the consumer with some form of copy and thinking about how our brand can encourage everybody to read more.

author I hadn't heard of: T.H.E. Public. Another seemed to show hundreds of orange-tinted Polaroids, which, a note suggested, represented the visitors to a certain library on a single day.

The next time, the rectangular "book" had been transformed by the short-hair into a single dominating P, made up of many squares. Over the course of the evening, it lost its smoothness and became pixelated. The pair seemed very pleased with themselves about this. And thus drank more. Which in turn pleased me. The short-hair then started counting the paving stones outside my bar. He came back with the number 400. Long-hair made notes. There was much talk of photographers and cranes and printing techniques that neither myself nor the long-hair fully understood; tight deadlines and incredible archives and a great deal of excitement.

But through it all, the word "public" came up again and again, almost as often as "Two more, please." It was as if they thought themselves responsible for the concept itself. But you know, I liked that. Because I too am a man of the public. And I say this with pride: some words still have power. That was the gift of the long-hair and the short-hair. They grew on me, it's true. And they always left a tip.

JAMES JOYCE
THE GOOD SOLDIER SCHWEIK
JAROSLAV HASEK
WHEN THE GOING WAS GOOD
Evelyn Waugh
Quatermass II
NIGEL KNEALE
SINISTER STREET
COMPTON MACKENZIE
Summer Lightning
P.G. Wodehouse
ARNOLD BENNETT
Riceyman Steps
WING LEADER
'Johnnie' Johnson
BHOWANI JUNCTION
John Masters
PRAY FOR THE WANDERER
KATE O'BRIEN
The Midwich Cuckoos
JOHN WYNDHAM
BRIDESHEAD REVISITED
Evelyn Waugh
UNDER THE NET
IRIS MURDOCH
THE TRESPASSER
D. H. LAWRENCE
Destination Chungking
Han Suyin
The Volcanoes Above Us
NORMAN LEWIS
Doctor Sally
P.G Wodehouse
LUCKY JIM
Kingsley Amis
Two Women
Alberto Moravia
The Month of September
Frédérique Hébrard
THE THURBER ALBUM
James Thurber
At Home
William Plomer
Lord of the Flies
William Golding
THE BRASS BOTTLE
F. ANSTEY
BEASTS AND SUPER BEASTS
'SAKI'
THE WHITE PEACOCK
D. H. LAWRENCE
AUGUST FOLLY
ANGELA THIRKELL
BRIGHT DAY
J. B. PRIESTLEY
THE PLAGUE
Albert Camus
THE DAY OF THE FOX
NORMAN LEWIS
SIR ARTHUR QUILLER-COUCH
SELECTED SHORT STORIES
The Case-Book of Sherlock Holmes
SIR ARTHUR CONAN DOYLE
In Search of England
H. V. MORTON
THOSE BARREN LEAVES
ALDOUS HUXLEY
THE HARP IN THE SOUTH
RUTH PARK
AARON'S ROD
D. H. LAWRENCE
A NARROW STREET
ELLIOT PAUL
THE PRIESTLEY COMPANION
A HANDFUL OF DUST
EVELYN WAUGH
KNIGHT WITH ARMOUR
Alfred Duggan
JOHN WYNDHAM
THE SEEDS OF TIME
A WORLD OF STRANGERS
Nadine Gordimer
ERIC LINKLATER
Juan in China
BEASTS AND SUPER BEASTS
'SAKI'
THE HEYDAY IN THE BLOOD
GERAINT GOODWIN
GREEKS AND TROJANS
REX WARNER
THE TRIAL
FRANZ KAFKA
MEMOIRS OF A MIDGET
WALTER DE LA MARE
THE CHINESE ROOM
VIVIAN CONNELL
THE LOVED ONE
EVELYN WAUGH
THE PLAGUE AND I
Betty MacDonald
TWO ADOLESCENTS
Alberto Moravia
VILLAGE SCHOOL
'MISS READ'
WUTHERING HEIGHTS
EMILY BRONTË
PENGUIN ISLAND
ANATOLE FRANCE
THE BLACK GIRL IN SEARCH OF GOD:
BERNARD SHAW
PETER WARING
FORREST REID
JOANNA GODDEN
SHEILA KAYE-SMITH
SUMMER HALF
ANGELA THIRKELL
ERIC LINKLATER
Juan in America
Prester John
JOHN BUCHAN
TWILIGHT IN ITALY
D. H. LAWRENCE
Little Boy Lost
MARGHANITA LASKI
THE WAR IN THE AIR
H. G. WELLS
NORDENHOLT'S MILLION
J. J. CONNINGTON
THE ARABIAN BIRD
CONSTANTINE FITZ GIBBON
McSORLEY'S WONDERFUL SALOON
JOSEPH MITCHELL
SYBIL
OR: THE TWO NATIONS
BENJAMIN DISRAELI
THE DOORS OF PERCEPTION and HEAVEN AND HELL
Aldous Huxley
THE LAST GRAIN RACE
ERIC NEWBY
LOVE FOR LYDIA
H. E. BATES
Kangaroo
D. H. LAWRENCE
BY LOVE POSSESSED
James Gould Cozzens
MAJOR THOMPSON LIVES IN FRANCE
Pierre Daninos
LUDWIG BEMELMANS
Life Class
I, CLAUDIUS
Robert Graves
CLOCHEMERLE-BABYLON
GABRIEL CHEVALLIER
Memoirs of Hadrian
MARGUERITE YOURCENAR
The Treasure of the Sierra Madre
B. TRAVEN
NOBLESSE OBLIGE
SELECTED CAUTIONARY VERSES
HILAIRE BELLOC
The King's General
Daphne du Maurier
SOFT ANSWERS
RICHARD ALDINGTON
The Death of the Heart
Elizabeth Bowen
The Mountain is Young
Han Suyin
THE TRESPASSER
D. H. LAWRENCE
WOMEN IN LOVE
D. H. LAWRENCE
THE STORY OF RAGGED ROBYN
OLIVER ONIONS
Lesley Blanch
THE WILDER SHORES OF LOVE
ROOM AT THE TOP
John Braine
A Damsel in Distress
P. G. Wodehouse
UNCLE FRED IN THE SPRINGTIME
JANE EYRE
CHARLOTTE
Rebecca
Daphne du Maurier
The World My Wilderness
Drinkers of Darkness
THE WHITE SOUTH
J. D. SALINGER
The Catcher in the Rye
ANDRÉ MIGOT
TIBETAN MARCHES
THE CRUISE OF THE 'NONA'
Aldous Huxley
EYELESS IN

Qq

Alan Fletcher + Jamie Jauncey

Alan Fletcher's diary

We were asked to keep a diary "as a written record of the process of creating the poster." That's a word-led request. So I've passed it on to my writer collaborator. My diary is visual. A collection of correspondence, notes, images and scribbles. A potential collage rather than a sequence of sentences. I don't think in a step-by-step fashion, or string things together like beads. I shuffle in backwards and look around.

Jamie Jauncey's diary

Quoyle clinched it for me. Awkward, eccentric, touchingly hopeless. The unlikely hero of Annie Proulx's *The Shipping News*. I saw his lumbering form the minute my eye landed on Q. One quirky, marginal character represented by another.

I pinned large sheets of paper to the wall and let them fill up with words like shrapnel from an exploded dictionary. Quoyle was joined by Quixote, and became a quizzical quinquagenarian. Quidditch and Quetzalcóatl conjured the fantastical. A quartet of quaggas picked their way queasily through a quagmire. And all the while, in the back of my mind, was the image of a snakelet emerging from an egg.

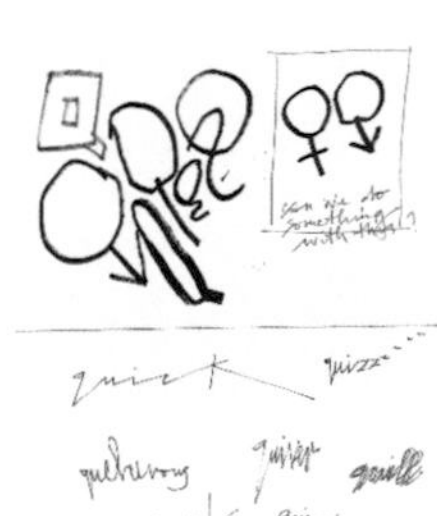

I felt I should explore further, delve back into alphabetical history. I liked *qoph*, the Phoenician monkey character with his descending tail. And *qoppa*, the abandoned Greek Q. I toyed with thoughts of QWERTY and the need to separate alphabetical partners to prevent typewriter keys from jamming.

The snake was still there.

I pondered Q's dependence on U, and its condition as one of the least-used letters in the alphabet. I doodled a quark travelling at high speed across a wall. A doleful queue of Qs waited at a bus stop. An upside-down Q made a face with a wavy quiff.

But the snake's egg wouldn't go away. So I drew it cracked, the snakelet emerging. Then began to add its neighbours, and realized that two letters before sat O, a perfect egg, while two letters later wriggled S, the full-grown snake.

It was time to contact my design partner Alan Fletcher. I sent him a long email explaining my thoughts. Back came some black-and-white images and the gnomic reply:

QUORUM

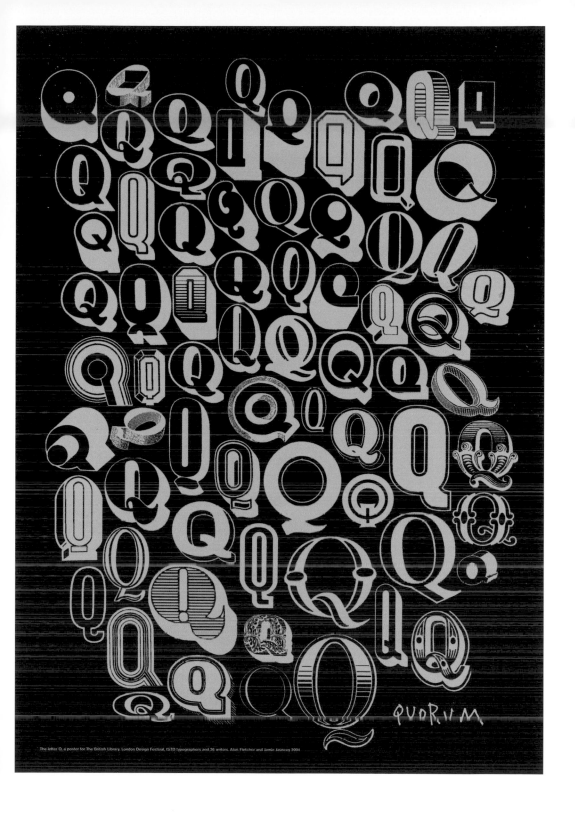

The letter Q, a poster for The British Library, London Design Festival, ISTD typographers and 26 writers. Alan Fletcher and Jamie Jauncey 2004

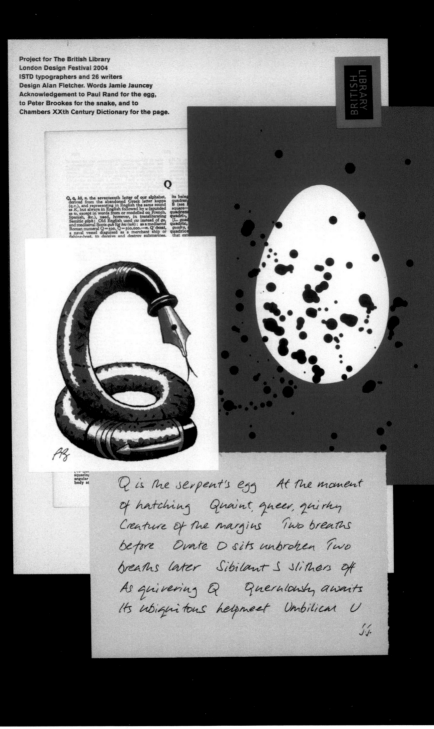

Project for The British Library
London Design Festival 2004
ISTD typographers and 26 writers
Design Alan Fletcher. Words Jamie Jauncey
Acknowledgement to Paul Rand for the egg,
to Peter Brookes for the snake, and to
Chambers XXth Century Dictionary for the page.

BRITISH
LIBRARY

Q

Q, q, *kū*, *n.* the seventeenth letter of our alphabet, derived from the abandoned Greek letter koppa (q.v.), and representing in English the same sound as *K*, but always in English followed by *u* (sounded as *w*, except in words from or modelled on French, Spanish, &c.), used, however, in transliterating Semitic *qōph*: Old English used *cw* instead of *qu*, and mediaeval Scots *quh* for *hw* (*wh*): as a mediaeval Roman numeral Q = 500, Q̄ = 500,000.—*n.* Q'-boat, a naval vessel disguised as a merchant ship or fishing-boat, to deceive and destroy submarines.

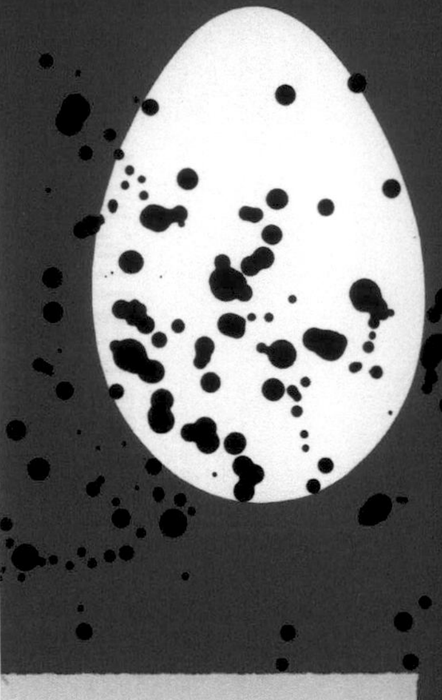

Q is the serpent's egg At the moment
of hatching Quaint, queer, quirky
Creature of the margins Two breaths
before Ovate O sits unbroken Two
breaths later Sibilant S slithers off
As quivering Q Querulously awaits
Its ubiquitous helpmeet Umbilical U

J.J.

Designer: Alan Fletcher
"…he has been depicted as the man who took all that serious less-is-more, form-follows-function dogma and somehow found a way to, well, relax."
Jeremy Myerson, design writer

Writer: Jamie Jauncey
Jamie Jauncey wears a cupboard full of hats: one for working as a writer with people in business, one as a novelist for adults and children, one as a musician.

"You do the inside and I do the outside. Put another way, you do the counter – the white bit – and I do the letter – the black bit. My letter is formed/conditioned by your counter. Thus I await your word, words, wordage. Because this will influence whether my letter will be fat, bold, thin or condensed."

Gruff of voice and sparing of word, Alan is the only person I have known who, when asked if that is Alan at the other end of the line, can reply: "Possibly." No wonder he chose Q.

His preferred means of communicating was by handwritten fax. I began to respond in kind. It lent character and a sense of comradeship to our deliberations. Soon I had in front of me a beautiful drawing of a large egg and a fat coiled serpent, with text in between. I started refining my words until they read like this:

Q is the serpent's egg / At the moment of hatching / Quaint, queer, quirky / Creature of the margins / Two breaths before / Ovate O sits unbroken / Two breaths later / Sibilant S slithers off / As quivering Q / Querulously awaits / Its ubiquitous helpmeet / Umbilical U.

Alan's thoughts had moved on too, away from the literal. Now we had a speckled egg and a nibbed pen like a half-coiled, half-rearing snake. Beneath was an empty space for the words, which he asked me to hand-write. He'd been getting me into training with the faxes, I realized.

He also wanted to explore an idea of his own: the noun of multitude for Q. He faxed me a sheet of Qs, crowded and jostling, like birds in a cage. I wanted to hear them squawk and screech and whistle and sing. I wrote a lot of words (too many) about this multitude. Alan had in mind just one. From my gabble he plucked *quorum*. We had coined a new collective noun. A quorum of Qs.

We were never going to argue the toss about our respective ideas. We simply agreed to do both and let the panel decide.

It was our gift to them. A quandary.

Rr

Michael Johnson + Roger Horberry

6-4-04 'Kinel – 26 want me to do a poster for London Design Week to be shown at the British Library. I'm flattered.

14-5-04 Got the design partner's mail today – I'm paired with Michael Johnson. Q has Alan Fletcher. Now I'm just freaked out. Does everyone feel like this?

20-5-04 Got my British Library reader's card this morning. What a palaver. The session started at 10 so I got the hugely expensive early train, supposedly getting me in to Kings Cross at 9.45. No chance, it was half an hour late getting into York (badgers undermining a signal box in the Darlington area or something equally daft), then more delays at every opportunity. I finally get to town only about 20 minutes before the cheap train would have got me there. Anyway, caught the arse-end of the presentations, got my card, chatted with the 26 folks, looked at some achingly beautiful books… and then went home. Just the 450-mile round trip. I hadn't given any thought to how the British Library might differ from a local equivalent; it seems you have to order books up from the vaults, ideally days ahead of time, which are then delivered to a reading room of your choice by lab-coated retainers. And basically I was too knackered and brain-fried to start. Plus I still have no idea what to do.

22-5-04 Looked around the second-hand bookshop I've walked past a hundred times but never been in. Loads of stuff on typography but strangely enough flicking through a heap of mouldering over-priced design tomes didn't help. On the way home I thought about John Simmons's maxim of "take yourself to work" and his belief in the power of poetry. Maybe I could do a poem about R; I picked it in the first place because it's somehow my letter, so it's personal from the off. But I haven't written a poem since I was 14.

23-5-04 How about not having *any* writing on the poster? Just do something ultra-confident based on information design, perhaps mapping the occurrence of the letter R in a particular text? Nah – it's been done.

As I sped the Police sedan downtown one thought kept pounding in my head – why had the thief pulled this heist? He could have done a bank job, maybe gutted the Museum. Still, I had to hand it to him, this was something that would go down in the annals of villainy. I hit the gas and let my mind go blank as I bucketed down 77th to the scen
BLIND
As I got close I could make out a mass of Police vehicles. This was definitely the place. Ahead of me beat cops filled the sidewalk. I stopped the sedan and walked up. I could see Captain Goudy and his sleazy sidekick Typo shaking with disbelief. They knew this was a tough one. I decided to play it cool.
EMBASSY ENVELOPES
APOLLO
VELMA DUNNE
"JOY OF LIV
"DON'T GO
WE BUY AND SE SLIGHTLY USE
"So, Chief, what's the deal?"
Goudy eyeballed me. If I was cool, he was ice cold. "Nuthin you need to know, Tschichold. This ain't Homicide business. Get back uptown an' chase some stiffs."
"I just thought you could use some help. Y'know, a new set of eyes."
Goudy paused then sighed. "What the hell. Typo, show this bad penny the scene." He shuffled away, shaking his head. Suddenly he looked old.
Inside the Bibliotech, police tape showed the spot. The thief was on the ball – he'd used the one skylight not connected to the Station. Lab boys busily dusted, hunting dabs, but the place was clean.
"Well?" I knew, but I wanted Typo to tell me anyway.
"It seems someone got in late last night and was gone by dawn. He knew what he wanted. Only took one consonant, but all the books have been cleaned out – not one left untouched." Typo paused. "How he did it, we don't know – yet – but we'll get him." We both knew he didn't sound too convinced.
DA Bodoni ambled up. "Say Tschichold, how you doing? Ain't seen you since the Clio case. We nailed 'em good, huh?"
Yeah, I thought, we nailed 'em good – and you walked away with the fame. Happens all the time. "What you got?" I asked politely.
"Evey R taken, 'cept that one." He gestued towads a single capital that lay on the floo, lost and folon. "We've been avoiding paticula wods all day, you too I expect."
He was ight. I'd been watching what I said since I'd head the APB ealie that moning. Now I could speak easy, at least fo the moment.
Bodoni was still talking. "...but we can't keep that up fo eve. Soon the pess will be hee and the entie wold will know. The Mayo will want a colla quick, that's fo sue."
The situation looked gim. The city couldn't go aound avoiding one missing lette all yea. Petty soon we'd stat looking idiculos. Oadsigns, newspapes, boadcasts and even the theate wee all affected by this deadful cime. We needed a apid esult. I pondeed.
"Did the ciminal leave any mak?" I enquied.
"Only this" eplied Typo, gestuing at a piece of lower case abandoned beneath the skylight. Staight away I ecognised the typeface and somewhee in my weay cop bain a light bulb lit up bight and clea.
This was the wok of P, evil typogaphic genius and all ound bad egg. I'd head he'd boken out of the pen and was planning evenge. He was one bitte lette – jealous of R's gaceful leg and looking fo vengeance. This had his fingepints all ove it – actually it didn't but you get my dift.
As I walked by to my ca my mind was buzzing. If P was ou man then the chase would be had. Life wouldn't be the same again until all the puloined Rs wee secuely back in the Bibliotech.
R
THE Spot BA G ILL
As I oared away I knew I had to catch him, and fast.
Story: Roger Horberry Design: johnson banks Illustration: Neal Fox

25-5-04 I was reading my daughter Lotte a bedtime story – *Letterland* – and it made me think about doing something on the secret lives of letters. Give them characters and write a little piece on how they all hate each other and do nothing but bitch among themselves – a bit like *The Office*. Mother-in-law Sue offered me a dip in her hot tub (how North Yorkshire does that sound?) and while reclining I pitched it to brother-in-law Leo, but he said it was crap. Oh well.

Then I thought about the three Rs and doing something with that. Except I wouldn't have arithmetic as my third R, I'd have response,

Designer: Michael Johnson
Michael Johnson is author of the best-selling *Problem Solved: A primer in design and communication* (Phaidon Press, 2002). He co-curated the Rewind exhibition at the Victoria and Albert Museum and was D&AD President in 2003.

Writer: Roger Horberry
Roger is a writer and consultant with a background in branding, design and the web. He lives in Yorkshire with Lucy, Lotte and George. He makes CDs of strange music. He even manages to sell a few.

of the letter R from all the books in the city library and doing it in the style of James Ellroy, with a hardboiled noir LA cop circa 1950. Well, I like a challenge. Rattled it off in under an hour. Turned out rather well.

11-6-04 Señor Johnson, he say yes! Now all we have to do is sort out how best to illustrate it…

29-6-04 Michael sent me a rough of the proposed layout – sort of graphic-novel-type frames included within a bolshy great big R, with the text to flow around it. Looks great. He has an illustrator in mind. As we've no money this will rely on Michael's considerable charm to bring about.

Ss

Erik Spiekermann + Howard Fletcher

A diary beginning with S

Howard: To me, the purpose of a poster is to promote (that's what 30 years in advertising does to you), so my instinct was to treat the letter S as a product. What are its benefits? What can it do for you?

That's why I was initially sceptical about the British Library connection. It all seemed wordy and worthy. I wasn't sure how academia could help find a proposition to push the letter S.

During the learned library tour I strayed to a case displaying original handwritten Lennon & McCartney lyrics. "She Said She Said." Ah, so S crops up a lot. It's obviously a useful letter...

Erik: I was pleased we had the letter S because I love it. I was also flattered because I'm Spiekermann and I use it frequently. At the same time I was scared because S is one of the most difficult letters to design. It's the letter that allows least licence with its shape as there's not much you can take away without losing its meaning. You can reduce other letters to a skeleton, but not S.

It's also truly onomatopoeic: it looks the way it sounds. It's the snake – it hisses and it looks like a hiss.

As I'd been given a British Library reader's card I thought I might as well see what the place had to offer. I typed "the letter S" into the on-screen search box. Just one title came up, "The Drone in the Ballroom," a poem written in 1829 "without any intervention of the letter S." Its author, the Reverend F. Newman, apparently believed that S, "so prevalent in the English language," was "injurious to vocalised music." Hardly a strong selling point.

In an email to Howard I suggested he look up "Ode minus sigma" written without the letter S by Pindar in 500 BC. I suggested we simply leave out the Ss from any text he cared to compose.

Back at the library, typing "alphabet" was more fruitful. In "The Alphabet Abecedarium," I discovered that more words in modern English begin with S than any other letter. I thought of doing the opposite of the good Rev and composing a poem using S words exclusively. We'd obviously have plenty to choose from.

Your perm is all hot, he cried.

S changes things.
It can make a kid skid.
It can make a coot scoot.
It can make a table stable.
It can even make a mall small.
And there's no better way
to make ink sink.

Your sperm is all shot, she cried.

S changes things.
It can make a kid skid.
It can make a coot scoot.
It can make a table stable.
It can even make a mall small.
And there's no better way
to make ink sink.

S changes things.
It can make a kid skid.
It can make a coot scoot.
It can make a table stable.
It can even make a mall small.
And there's no better way
to make ink sink.

After a scribble or two, this proved problematic. Should sexy slut Susie suck saveloys or sausages? Anyway, it was sounding too much like a tongue-twister.

On the phone between Berlin and London, we talked about ideas leaving out the letter S. We agreed that this might be a bit obvious and was too close to the "Lost Consonants" series of cartoons in the *Guardian*. Howard told me about his discoveries at the British Library.

The apple crumble and custard in the British Library café was especially good. I'd also concluded that S could perhaps be positioned as the alphabet's most powerful letter. Placed at the end of many words, it has the power to multiply. It also has the power to change sex. And it's one of the most frequently occurring letters within the bodies of English words.

In my Berlin studio, Howard and I discussed creative routes based on the power of S. We saw how placing an S in front of many words completely changes their meaning. A few well-placed Ss can transform a phrase or sentence.

The innocuous "I'm having a little wine" becomes "I'm shaving a little swine." And "'Hark,' he cried, 'don't go to Cuba'" transforms into "'Shark,' she cried, 'don't go to scuba.'" A kipper with a pear ends up as the much more interesting skipper with a spear. There seemed to be no limit to the power of S. It can make a hake shake and a mother smother. We clearly had many poster possibilities, without having to make a tart start or a hag shag.

We chose our favourite before and after line, with and without Ss, and Howard wrote a short piece of text to define the idea further. I then had the task of making the concept work in print. I arrived at the layout by looking at the words closely; I had to show two different messages in the same medium so there weren't too many choices. A series of strategically placed folds helped.

Designer: Erik Spiekermann
Erik Spiekermann is an information architect, type designer (of Meta and Officina, among others) and author. He was the founder of MetaDesign (1979) and FontShop (1988). He is president of ISTD and lives in Berlin and San Francisco.

Writer: Howard Fletcher
Howard writes to change opinions about products, companies and issues. He has no plans to write novels, poetry or anything non-commercial. With an advertising background (and three D&AD pencils) he adopts a campaigning approach to business writing.

As Erik worked on the type, I thought about my discoveries at the British Library. I'd found a strange poem, "S" by Ted Hughes (something about snakes). I'd found Fanny Craddock's *A Cook's Essential Alphabet* with vital information on salsify. And I'd come across the classic song "I'd like to change the alphabet, baby, so I'll be closer to U." All in all, despite my initial doubts, it had been an enriching experience.

Looking at fonts, I needed to find one that worked with the idea of two sentences saying opposite things in almost the same way. All the letters had to take up the same width. I chose INFO, a face I designed some years ago for signage systems. The Office version is slightly reminiscent of typewriting – the M is narrow and the I is wide so they fit the same space.

I reversed the type out of black to make the poster stand out against a light wall. White was the obvious colour for the safe, neutral message, while the more dangerous intervention of the letter S just had to be challenging, attention-seeking red.

We ended up with a poster that was a true collaboration, a combination of removing the S from words and adding the S to words. In an impactful way, we demonstrated how the letter S has the power to change things.

My favourite moment of the project came after we'd sorted the poster, when I told Erik about the handwritten lyrics of "She Said She Said." He grabbed his *Revolver* CD from the shelf and we shared some sixties nostalgia. Another example of the power of S. "He Aid He Aid" just wouldn't have sounded the same.

Tt

Henrik Kubel + John Spencer

5 August 2003 [Email from Tom Lynham] Hi John, Hope you are blooming. You know that I have been clubbing together with other writers to form a new association to promote the wonder of words in business and design.

Well, we have named ourselves 26 and it's all happening with bells on. We are launching at the Design Council on September 25 @ 6–8 p.m. as part of the London Design Festival 2003 sponsored by Penguin and other luminaries.

As one of my staunchest supporters for many years, I would love to invite you.

Tickets are extremely limited so please let me know either way as soon as possible. Big and best. T

6 August Hi Tom, Fantastic. Love to come. It's in the diary. Rock 'n' roll. J

25 September Inspiring launch. Still amazes me that anyone needs to be persuaded of the importance of writing in design. Claimed the letter X as mine.

4 November [Email from Margaret Oscar] Hi John, Unfortunately the letter X has been taken. Would you like to choose another? Me

5 November Hi Margaret, T is for Tom, my son, who's terrific.
I'll have T. Ta. J
Hi John, T is yours. Cute. My son is also called Tom. Me

20 April 2004 Email invitation from 26 to work on a poster celebrating the letter T.

6 May Brief received.

13 May Poster design partners revealed.

20 May Introduction to the resources of the British Library.

25 May Lunch meeting with Henrik Kubel to discuss first thoughts. Bacon sandwiches. No expense spared.

John's Images

Tom
The inspiration for my choice of the letter T. This photograph was taken of my son when he was seven. Funny how kids are proud of losing their teeth. Doubtless, though, their pride is fuelled by the excitement of getting a quid for each and a message from the Tooth Fairy written with Dad's left hand.

Twig
September 1994, and a walk in the National Trust's Claremont Landscape Garden revealed Tom's surprisingly early interest in letterforms. Wow, his mum thought, as he picked up a twig and said, 'T for Tom'. The alphabet is everywhere. I like the letter T. So simple. So matter-of-fact.

Twin
Thomas is the Greek form of the Aramaic name Te'oma which meant twin. The ultrasound scan is a marvel of science. For me it symbolises the miracle of life. And the tragedy of Holly's stillbirth.

Thailand
Buddhas, temples, a friendly monk, elephants, tuk-tuks, Bangkok traffic jams, longboats, Phi Phi Island, a tree house, turquoise sea, a massage. Monopoly, noodles, cocktails, Singha beer. A holiday with friends. A postcard home.

Tag
I love graffiti's rawness. Its boldness. Its humour. Its anger. Its devilishness. Of course, much of it is nothing more than vandalism. But at its breathtaking best, it's a public statement of private thoughts. Tom's a graffiti enthusiast but not a practitioner (as far as I know). This is Henrik's tag. The Devil is looking over his shoulder at Gutenberg's Bible. A nice touch, we thought.

Tyke
The parents of 'little tykes' will be familiar with the relentless task of removing mucky handprints from walls, doors and just about everywhere else. And they don't need much encouragement to make their mark on paper. Handprints are a powerful universal symbol. They say, 'This is me. I am here'. This is Tom's handprint.

Try
Not many people know this. In the early days of rugby the only way of scoring was to kick the ball between the posts. Touching the ball down over the goal line, or the touchline as it was called, allowed a team to try for a conversion kick. That's why a try is called a try. This illustration, courtesy of Mary Evans Picture Library, dates from 1897.

Henrik's Images

Tschichold
Jan Tschichold's greatest contribution to the history and practice of 20th century typography was to demonstrate the importance of getting the details right. And to do it with elegance. Tschichold introduced 'elementary' design principles. He maintained that typography is shaped by functional requirements and that the aim of typographic layout is communication, for which it is the graphic medium. Tschichold also believed that communication must appear in the shortest, simplest, most penetrating form, and, for typography to serve social ends, its ingredients need internal organisation (ordered content) and external organisation (the typographic material properly related). Tschichold stressed the importance of the photograph and of the unprinted areas of paper. He believed in the 'correctness' of sanserif typefaces and proposed that type could be set obliquely or vertically. Tschichold championed the adoption of standardised DIN (Deutsche Industrie Normen) paper sizes, such as A4 for writing paper. He rejected the use of all ornament other than squares, circles and triangles, and even these were only to be used when they were rooted in the overall construction. Tschichold developed and refined his thinking in the most important single document of the Modern Movement, his book 'Die Neue Typographie', which was published in 1928.

Type tray
Between 1998 and 2000 I was a student on the MA Communication Art & Design Course at the Royal College of Art in London, and a frequent user of the college typography workshop run by the prolific master of letterpress Alan Kitching. The workshop houses a large collection of metal type. Baskerville 11pt was my favourite with Baskerville Italic 14pt for captions. I found this diagram of a standard type tray in the workshop. Historically, the working typesetter used two trays, one contained the majuscules or capitals and the other contained the minuscules, better known as lower case. That's the origin of the expressions upper case and lower case.

Two
The letter T was the 22nd and last letter of the Phoenician alphabet. It was known by the Semitic name taw which meant mark. Taw's shape was usually cruciform, like a + sign or extended lengthways like the Christian cross. In our alphabet, the letter T is the 20th letter and, perhaps surprisingly, the second most frequently used after the letter E. (Incidentally, the letter A is third). I discovered this in a book recommended by the ISTD, International Society of Typographic Designers called 'The Alphabet', written by David Sacks and published by Hutchinson in 2003. I have chosen two things to represent the number two; a woodblock number from our studio's extensive wood type collection and 'The Express Ready Reckoner', a book that contains tens of thousands of numbers. In fact, that's all it contains. It was typeset in metal using a variety of fonts and printed in letterpress on bible paper.

T-sign
Sign language uses the hands and fingers to form each letter of the alphabet. The T-sign is very reminiscent of the sporting 'time out' gesture. In America a different configuration is used where the hand is closed and the thumb positioned between the third and fourth fingers. It seems to me that this is a much stronger and more emotive gesture. We all carry the alphabet in our hands. That's amazing!

Type
The Dutch claim that the inventor of movable type and printing was not Johann Gutenberg of Mainz but Laurens (or Lourens) Janszoon Coster of Haarlem. It was he, allegedly, who developed the technique of printing with moveable type between 1423 and 1440, years before Gutenberg printed his 'magnum opus', the 42-line Bible. (42 is a reference to the number of lines of type on the page.) Jan Middendorp, who lives and works in Ghent, makes this claim in his recent, and highly recommended, 350-page book on Dutch typography, [illegible]. The book is published by 010 Publishers. In my search for the truth I discovered 'The Justification of Johann Gutenberg', a novel by Blake Morrison that was published in 2000 by Chatto and Windus, London. It is a brilliant, light-hearted read and gives an insight into the man who I believe changed history. I have chosen to feature a spread from Gutenberg's printed Bible together with his portrait. These images were kindly supplied by the British Library where the Bible is on permanent display.

Typewriter
The world's first personal computer! This is a Remington 12 which was manufactured from 1878. According to the gold foil lettering on its black enamel case, this model was made at Ilion, New York in 1934. It has an engraved identification number, LK 43058, and a mark of quality with the inscription 'To save time is to lengthen life'. It can print in three colours; black, red and white. This 'Rolls Royce' of a typewriter was rescued from a rubbish tip in Jeffrey Street, Camden, in the summer of 2004. The Remington has recently been cleaned and polished and is now sitting beside its 'Italian cousin', the dusty green Olivetti Lettera 22 which was produced in Britain between 1954 and 1964. Both machines are on display in the A2-GRAPHICS/SW/HK design and typography studio. They are greatly admired.

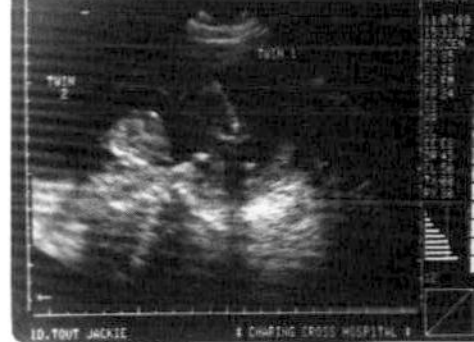

Research, pictures, words & design by John Spencer, Spencerlin Box Limited & Henrik Kubel, A2-GRAPHICS/SW/HK, London 2004
The typeface used for the captions is part of the Book Serie designed by Henrik Kubel

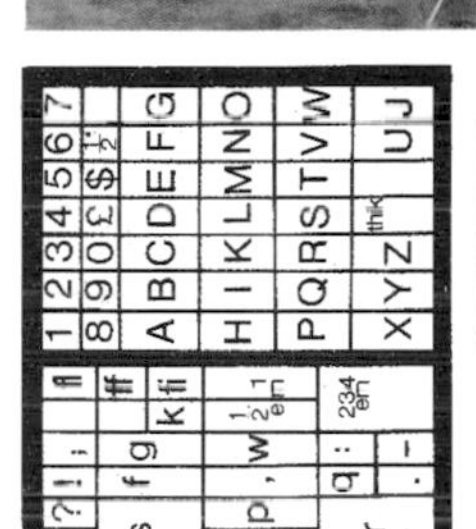

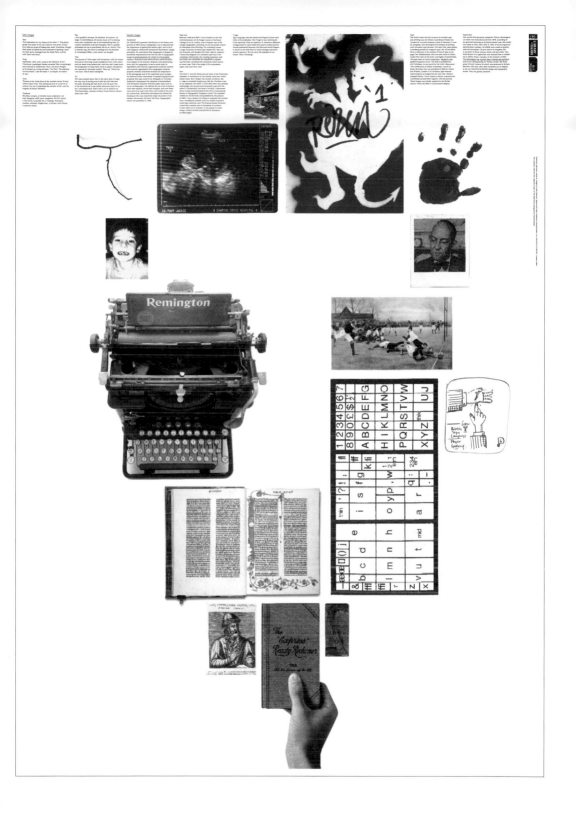

Type

The Dutch claim that the inventor of movab
and printing was not Johann Gutenberg of M
Laurens (or Lourens) Janszoon Coster of Haa
he, allegedly, who developed the technique
with moveable type between 1423 and 1440
Gutenberg printed his 'magnum opus', the 4
(42 is a reference to the number of lines of ty
page.) Jan Middendorph, who lives and wor
makes this claim in his recent, and highly re
320-page book on Dutch typography, 'abcdu
fghijklmnopqrstuvwxyz'. The book is publis
010 Publishers. In my search for the truth I
'The Justification of Johann Gutenberg', a no
Blake Morrison that was published in 2000
and Windus, London. It is a brilliant, light-h
read and gives an insight into the man who
changed history. I have chosen to feature a s
Gutenberg's printed Bible together with his
These images were kindly supplied by the Br
Library where the Bible is on permanent dis

Designer: Henrik Kubel
Henrik Kubel graduated in 1997 from Denmark's Design School in Copenhagen and received an MA from the Royal College of Art in London in 2000. In 1999 he founded A2-GRAPHICS/SW/HK with fellow graduate Scott Williams.

Writer: John Spencer
John Spencer is creative director and joint owner of Spencer du Bois. Most of the design consultancy's work is for not-for-profit organizations and aims to challenge attitudes and change the way people think.

We agreed design concept: create a virtual T that's formed from a seemingly random collection of images. Eclectic. Emotive. Engaging.

We decided each to research our own images. Will be interesting to see how the poster turns out since we're coming at it from different directions. My inspiration is personal: each image will be intimately associated with my son Tom. Henrik's, while personal, is very much influenced by the development of printing and his passion for all things typographic.

24 June Meeting to compare notes, agree the image subjects and test them against the concept. Looking good. Agreed to meet up in two to three weeks with the final images.

25 June Hi Henrik, Good to see you yesterday. Here are the 14 images we've agreed on:
Yours 42-line Bible, number 22, Remington typewriter, type tray, photo of your girlfriend, hands (in shape of T).
Mine Photo of Tom, T twig, twins scan, rugby try card, television, river Thames, Thai Buddha, tag (graffiti).
Speak soon. J

Hi John, Thanks for the list. It's all looking very promising, I think. Let's meet Tuesday 20. Best wishes. Henrik

14 July
Dear John, I am working away on the images and think that I have got them all. Here's a JPEG of the current status. I am working on the text too, and looking forward to meeting you to discuss further. Maybe we meet in my studio on Monday? Let me know. Best wishes. Henrik

21 July
Last meeting before artwork. Decided on photographic production process. Rough layout agreed. Draft text is currently being prepared. We decided to write extended captions and to make the words as informative as possible. It seems to us that this approach complements and at the same time contrasts with our choice of images. We've attempted to give them meaning beyond the subjective.

Uu

Peter Dawson + Dan Germain

Peter's diary: U what?!
As a creative team, we first met at the briefing on the British Library's resources. We knew our letter would be U by then, but our direction and idea? Difficult one.

As we sat in the auditorium of the British Library conference centre, Michelle Brown, manuscripts curator, introduced us to examples from the collection. Seeking comfort in the illuminated manuscripts being displayed, we found our inspiration: the universe.

Early maps of the universe had turned images of the sky at night into beautiful illustrations; the idea of creating our own twenty-first century version was the start of our creative toil. Just as well: with over 180,000,000 artefacts in the British Library, it could have taken some time before we stumbled upon our inspiration.

The question then became: how do we fit the universe into an A0 poster? And what do we say about it? Dan took up the gauntlet and started researching the background to our letter. We discovered that U is believed to have emerged from the Phoenician alphabet around 800 BC. In his essay "In praise of vowels," Ernst Jünger described U as the most "difficult vowel to characterize," evoking as it does "the dark force of being – the secrets of procreation and death."

We had agreed that our direction was U for universe, but how could we bring the piece back to the British Library? Initial exploration led us to the idea that the universe knows no boundaries, and then we moved on to the theme of universal knowledge with "knowledge knows no boundaries." The final idea was that the British Library contains a universe of knowledge within its walls. The themes of knowledge and learning involved with libraries and other institutions worked perfectly with our ideas and our copy was soon created.

We had been discussing the aesthetic quality of our piece for nearly as long as we had been researching the universe. We explored a "black" aesthetic to try and communicate the vastness of space, but we also needed to visualize the concept of information and data to tie in with the library. I wanted to work with the themes of walls and containment using varying scales and multiple layers to create a feeling of depth.

My approach was to create a graphic British Library by presenting the different floor levels of the actual building. These would be

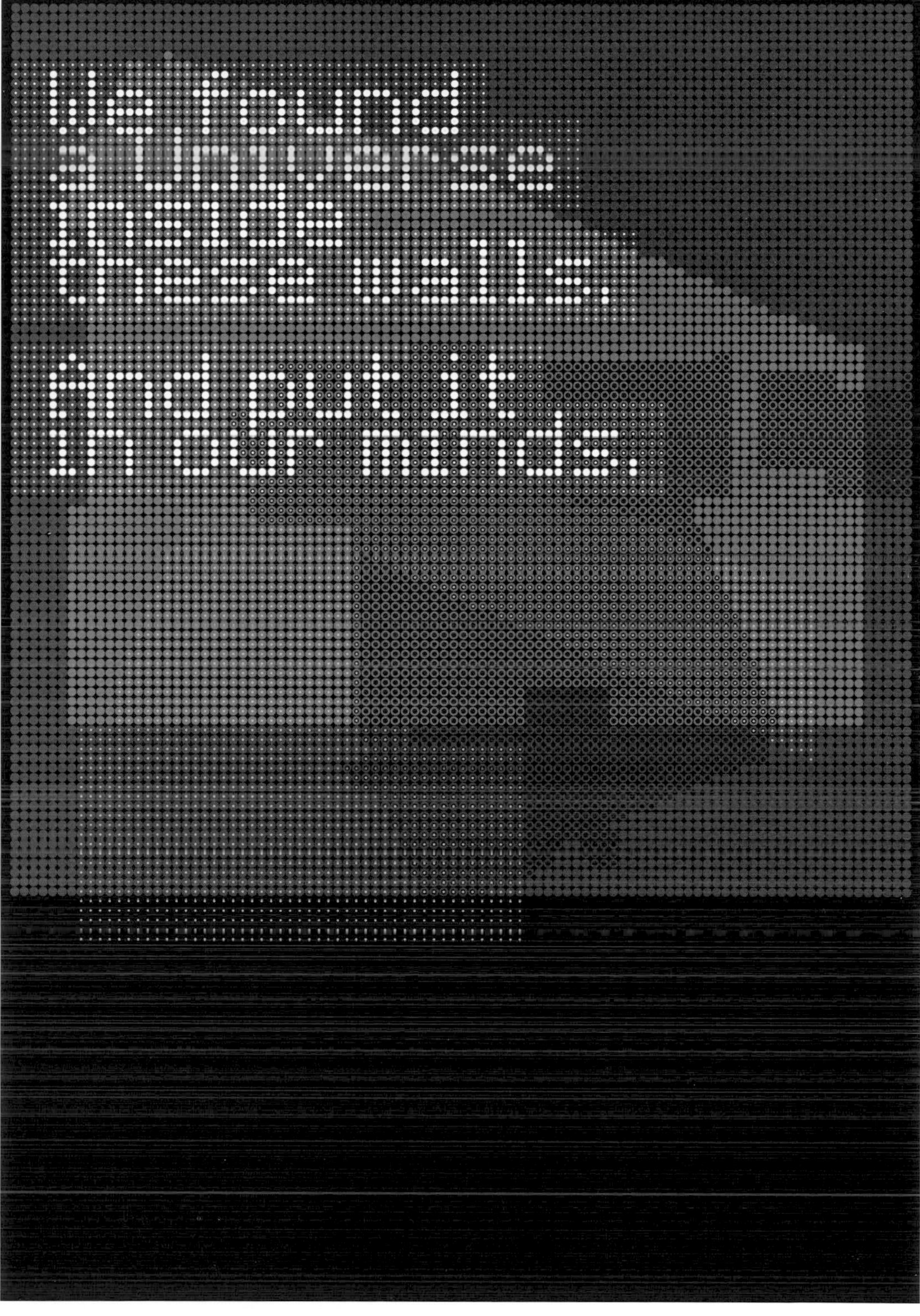
We found
these walls.
And put it
in our minds.

Designer: Peter Dawson
Creative director, founding partner of Grade Design in London and chair of publications on the ISTD council, Peter has also held part-time lecturing posts on typography and design at Kingston University and London College of Printing.

Writer: Dan Germain
Dan has worked at innocent drinks since the company started. His responsibilities include copywriting, creative stuff and drinking any leftover smoothies.

abstracted and recomposed over and against each other. Having obtained detailed drawings of each floor, I set out to draw their core features on the computer. Once master outlines of each level had been created, they would be recreated entirely from type, using the typefaces Foundry Plek/Flek, designed by The Foundry.

Foundry Plek/Flek are based on a dot-matrix grid system, when laid over each other, the two fonts synchronize. This seemed an appropriate way of referring to past methods of data storage and transfer. Using the typeface and methodology allowed me to experiment with overlays and mix the weights to produce varying effects. With the centre of the underlying dot matrices remaining fixed, I was able to introduce Dan's text into the design as if it were embedded in the fabric of the British Library building itself.

By striking a balance between legibility and illustration, we hope to convey that a universe does indeed exist within these walls.

Dan's diary: All about U

We were lucky, Pete and me. We got in there early and nabbed U, which has a million and one connotations. Unfortunately, we couldn't remember any of them, so we spent a little while scratching our heads and sending lots of emails arranging to go for beers where we hoped that crucial fourth pint would elicit a moment of magic.

But more about that later. Mainly because we never got to the beer bit. We met once, at the British Library, and we got on pretty well. We chatted about the letter U and there was one thing I kept coming back to. Admittedly, it's an easy thing to keep coming back to, seeing as it's so big and all-encompassing and scary if you think about it for too long. So we chose to talk about It, the Oneness, an expanse of Nothing filled with stars and cosmic gas and monkeys who chuck bones at big black oblongs from another dimension.

Yes, we chose to discuss the universe. It begins with U and it gave us an incredibly wide brief. But rather than rattle on about stars and Shatner, we thought we'd take a moment to marvel at the British Library, which blew me away when I visited it. You see, the last public library I went to was in a place called Stony Stratford when I was 11, and I've still got the Ian Rush autobiography that I borrowed that day (we moved away soon afterwards and the Buckinghamshire

library police never caught up with me in north Kent). So stepping into the British Library was a bit of a revelation.

You can see our poster on these pages, and read for yourself what we said about the universe and the British Library. And it's an amazing feeling, thinking about the billions of hours of study and intellectual struggle going on in that building next door to St Pancras station. It blows your mind, just like the universe. And Pete has made our poster a bit mind-blowing as well. I hope I complimented him when I said it was fit to grace a Kraftwerk album cover.

So that's what we did. Pete was terrific to work with, I love the fact that it looks and sounds great, and the pair of us have ordered personal prints so that we can show off to the grandkids one day. And we're going to have that beer, soon.

Lila Szagun + Stuart Delves

Convergence: The diary of V

Lila, 14 July 2004 "My diaries and notebooks lost in a sea of removal boxes..."

Stuart, 14 July "This diary is a fiction. It's retrospective; selective: piecing together a creative venture and partnership..."

We met once. In York (Yorvick to the Vikings) on 28 May. We had coffee and lunch and took a glimpse inside the Minster. We looked at typefaces and images. We swapped insights; agreed a few things. But that's jumping the gun...

Lila, 17 May "Just writing to say hallo since we have been teamed up for the poster exhibition. As far as the poster is concerned I am really open-minded. I think a poem would be lovely, but anything is possible."

Stuart, 18 May "Here are my thoughts on V. They are a journey to a single word that is the essence of the letter. I suppose this is my diary. It's at first-draft stage – so, flexible and lots of room for improvement. What I was thinking: if the main body of the poster featured this one word, but also incorporated the journey taken to arrive at it. So the diary is part of the finished artefact. Process and product in one."

Lila, 21 May "I share your impressions in the sense that many V-words have something really unique or special about them. It is quite a seductive letter in some ways. I suppose when it comes down to it, it is all about the letter's physique, the two stems converging, thereby giving the impression of channelling energy (read in David Sacks about the man who believed the V-sign channelled cosmic energy). So, in my design I would like to use your story set into paragraphs at converging angles, eventually converging into the word 'verve.'"

Lila, 24 May "Had a couple of hours 'graphic-storming' yesterday and came up with this concept... this idea relates V to compasses, as used in Paolozzi's massive sculpture of Newton in front of the British Library. As in Blake's painting, a perfect V represents a symbolic tool for casting circles, representing the world of knowledge.

Number 22 *V le voyage*

vivienne

Verve

Graphically, V is so balanced, so elegant. A typeface can render it symmetrical, but classically it gives the illusion of symmetry: the left stem being slightly thicker than the right

In German, it appropriates W in pronunciation. But then it was formerly the symbol of U and W is simply a ligature of V

What's in a letter? What does V mean to me?

V and writing: verb, verse, voice, vocabulary
verbal & visual – the twin engines of communication

Vulpine. Ah, the sound of V when followed by an
O or U: Vol-au-vent, Voodoo, Vouvray

Where would love be without the v? It adds the edge
Where would evil be?

My favourite V brand is La Vache qui rit:
an early memory of my mother explaining its
personality on the veranda in Phnom Penh
I think of neighbouring Vietnam
Land of Peace, icon of war
How like Mesopotamia

Stars, paintings, beauty: we come to Venice
Incomparable, city of dreams

Each a rosary of mantras
Sound seeds: the beginning: life

Vivacity: the sparkle in my children
in my beloved

Vivienne: Lady of the Lake. Or Vivienne Westwood even: here, at St. Pancras, amongst volumes of quiet contemplation, saying 'this is the place for students wanting inspiration'. Students of fashion and students of life: the ephemeral and the evolving intertwined

Now there's a word

A great vivacity of ideas
Creative enthusiasm

From the Latin verba
plural of verbum

V's visually suggestive of deltas, wedges, pudenda. It's the letter of convergence. Also of divergence. V is a valley.

The newcomer, along with cousin J, ousting X from 22

What is its essence? The one word?

Or favourite V words: Voluptuous, Ventriloquist, Vellum, Velvet
Vajrayana: the diamond way

Then there are internal vs of course: unravel, ravishing, gravity, gravy

How about brand names? Volvo, Vittel, Volvic
VW: the ultimate triple V

What of the gods? Lame Vulcan (that right stem). Vishnu – the god of process. Venus (thanks Sandro). She shines brightly over the smokehouse kitchen across the way from our front porch

Beyond dreams: meaning. What's in a letter?

Mm, the life words: Viva, Vitality, Vulva, Now, surely, we're getting close: the slipped fish in the blue-tinged clay of vernix; the vibrancy of our genes reformed, entwined

A muse maybe? Vivienne:
vivid and vibrant with life

Life, Westwood, writing. Verve.

A special bent, vein, or talent
in writing

Old French: a form of expression,
vigour, whim

– word.

Designer: Lila Szagun
After graduating as a mature student from London College of Printing (now London College of Communication), Lila Szagun spent three months at MetaDesign in Berlin. Since October 2003, she has been working for Llewelyn Davies, an architecture and design firm in central London.

Writer: Stuart Delves
Stuart Delves (Z–A): married, 2 kids, co-founder Henzteeth; writer, Redpath Design; Centre Director, Arvon Foundation; advertising copywriter; impoverished playwright; Oxford, Clifton College, Amesbury School (correction penitentiary); dad MI6, mum too most likely; home birth Farnham, Surrey 1956.

I have used the word 'verve,' although I am not sure if this is the best word to use if we go down this route."

Stuart, 24 May "Thanks for this: your design is lovely and I feel there is the seed of something beautiful here. I like the compass idea and don't think it's opposed to the word 'verve.' I like the Blake reference and the Newton/British Library reference is good and pertinent.

"I do have a couple of concerns – I wouldn't want the finished article to smack in any way of the Masons, or indeed to be too mystical or intellectual. The journey (as I see it) includes the spiritual, the commercial, the literary, the emotional, the historical and the personal.

"I wonder if you'd envisaged any icons, e.g. VW, Venice, Vivienne Westwood? The juxtaposition of a bottle of Vittel and the BVM, for instance. (You mentioned convergence in your last email and I think this is a central aspect of V.)

"The commercial aspect is important as this is a brief for commercial writers and artists and it counterbalances anything mystical or spiritual. The converse is also true. We'll obviously have to meet!"

In York we discuss duality, dividing and converging, valleys and the youth of V. We agree on the Westwood boots – the *image, beating voluptuous stone goddess, deltas, Viking helmets and Virgin jet engines. We agree on the text moving as a meditation. We agree on "Le Voyage." We agree on playful Benguiat with gorgeous Es and Ed's whirling, spontaneous Edwardian. We agree not to spend the £4 to go into the nave of the Minster, bejesus!*

From then on it's detail, detail, detail.

Lila, 31 May "Contrary to my expectation we need to cut the text quite a bit. The viewer should be able to read comfortably from a little further away."

Stuart, 4 June "I prefer the version without legs. The way you've arranged the shoes is really good – the angle of the upright of the fallen shoe making a subtle V. The colours are really working too – the red brings power and is well complemented by the lime."

Acknowledgement
Many thanks to Wood & Wood for help with display and Eleanor Forster for the loan of her beautiful Vivienne Westwood shoes for the photo shoot.

Lila, 10 June "Have received your second draft. The two titles need sorting out properly – I'd like them to melt into each other, reinforcing the idea of converging ideas/words."

Stuart, 16 June "I've taken a couple of sentences out – down to about 400 words. Taken the bit out about midwives. I'll now leave this in your capable hands."

Lila, 2 July "Just wanted to let you know what is happening – have this idea to use acetate sheets with the type hung in front of another opaque poster sheet containing the graphic (i.e. background, shoes and the word 'verve')."

Lila, 12 July "I think we should keep in mind that the text of the poster will probably not be legible when printed in the book, so maybe we should use some of that..."

> *"Stars, paintings, beauty: we come to Venice. Incomparable, city of dreams.*
>
> *"Beyond dreams: meaning. What's in a letter? Each a rosary of mantras. Sound seeds: the beginning: life. Mm, the life words: viva, vitality, vulva. Now, surely, we're getting close: the slipped fish in the blue-tinged clay of vernix; the vibrancy of our genes reformed, entwined. Vivacity: the sparkle in my children; in my beloved.*
>
> *"A muse maybe? Vivienne: vivid and vibrant with life. Vivienne: Lady of the Lake. Or Vivienne Westwood even: here, at St Pancras, amongst volumes of quiet contemplation, saying 'This is the place for students wanting inspiration.' Students of fashion and students of life: the ephemeral and the evolving intertwined.*
>
> *"Life, Westwood, writing. Verve."*
>
> **Extract from "Le Voyage" by Stuart Delves**

Lila, 15 July "Looking at V now, I love that the piece is so open, inviting the viewer to ask why and what..."

And that was just the half of it.

Ww

Alan Kitching + Dan Radley

workshop **Friday 4 June 2004, Cleaver Street, Kennington**

Dan: The door to The Typography Workshop swings open and I'm greeted by a magnificent beard. A beard so full and bristly that it takes considerable willpower to stop staring at the chin of its wearer, my project partner, Alan Kitching RDI, AGI, FRCA, typographer, printmaker and letterpress guru.

Alan is fascinating. Apprenticed at 14 as a compositor in his local Darlington print works, he went on to have a prestigious and lucrative career in design. But at the age of 47, he threw everything in the air and returned to his passion, setting up his own letterpress workshop in Clerkenwell.

Both my parents were typographers, so it's a thrill to find myself in this Aladdin's cave. Evidence of Alan's craft is all around – cases of type, hand presses, composing sticks and stones, aromas of wood, ink and paper – a breath of fresh air in these homogeneous digital times.

He asks what I was hoping to get from this first meeting. I say I'm struggling with the open-endedness of the brief. I need a better mental impression of the target.

From the print room, Alan produces the biggest sheet of cardboard I've ever seen. Then he hands me a sketch of a first idea, beautifully simple and graphic: a capital W formed by two linked Vs, one of which is made up of words. He'll take half and I'll take half, echoing the collaborative nature of this project.

waffle **Tuesday 8 June, letter to Alan**

I scribble out my early thoughts in a letter. The first is to theme the poster around the great questions of life. Who? Why? What? Where? When?

I also consider writing in celebration of wood. Wood is good: it's enduring, sustainable and recyclable. Apparently "wood" is also jargon used by US editors for screaming headlines on tabloid newspapers.

Alan provides another starting point, a press clipping from *The Times* that says: "Most languages that call W 'double V' pronounce it as a V. English, by contrast, has a unique relationship with the letter. Usually used as a consonant (as in we), W also serves as a vowel in diphthongs, such as few and how; yet can be totally silent, as in wrist and answer. No wonder the English name the letter 'double U.'"

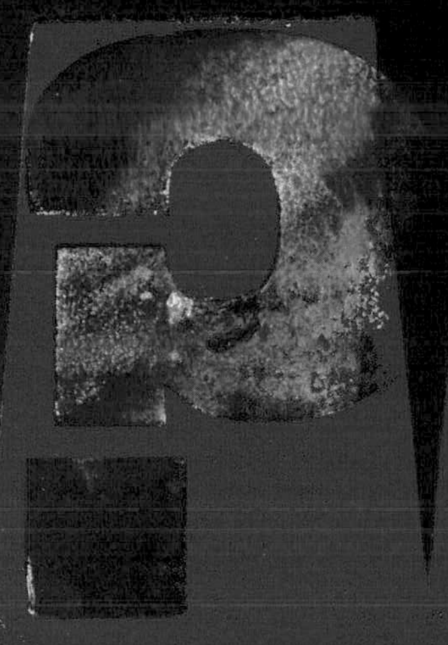

'WHO'S AFRAID OF
WYNKYN
DE WORDE,
THE DEMON PRINTER OF OLD FLEET STREET?'
CRIED ENGLAND'S ELITE.
INKY GAVE PEOPLE THE POWER TO LERNE
ENGLYSSHE AND FRENSSHE,
AND FYSSHYNGE WITH AN ANGLE.

'WHO'S AFRAID OF THE BIG BAD
DUBYA?'
SHUDDERS THE PLANET. BY GEORGE, I'M SCARED.
WASHINGTON STALKS IN
WESTMYNSTRE'S FLEECE
AND THE WILD
WEST
DREAMS ON IN THE EAST.

'WHO'S AFRAID OF
WAPPING
WOOD?'
SMIRKS THE TABLOID MAN
AT THE SYGNE OF THE SONNE.
ASYLUM-SEEKERS
AND BOOB-JOBS
ARE HIS WEAPONS OF MASS
DISTRACTION.
'AND WILL THE LAST PERSON
TO LEAVE BRITAIN PLEASE
TURN OUT THE LIGHTS?'
(IT WAS THE SONNE WOT WON IT.)

'WHY ARE YOU AFRAID
OF MY BIG, BAD
QUESTIONS?'
ASKS THE WYSE CHYLDE
OF THRE YERE OLDE.
WHO
AM I?
WHERE
AM I FROM?
WHAT
IS LOVE?
WHICH
CAME FIRST?
'ORANGE' OR
'ORANGES'
AND, IF THERE'S A GOD,
WHY
ALL THE
SUFFERING?'

'WHO'S AFWAID OF THE VOICED
BILABIAL SPIWANT?'
ASKS THE DANDY CHAT-SHOW HOST
BABIES AREN'T. WA-WA,
THEY CRY.
GUITARISTS AREN'T. WA-WA,
THEY REPLY.
AND AS FOR THE WASCAWY WABBIT:
W-W-W!
THAT'S ALL FOLKS!

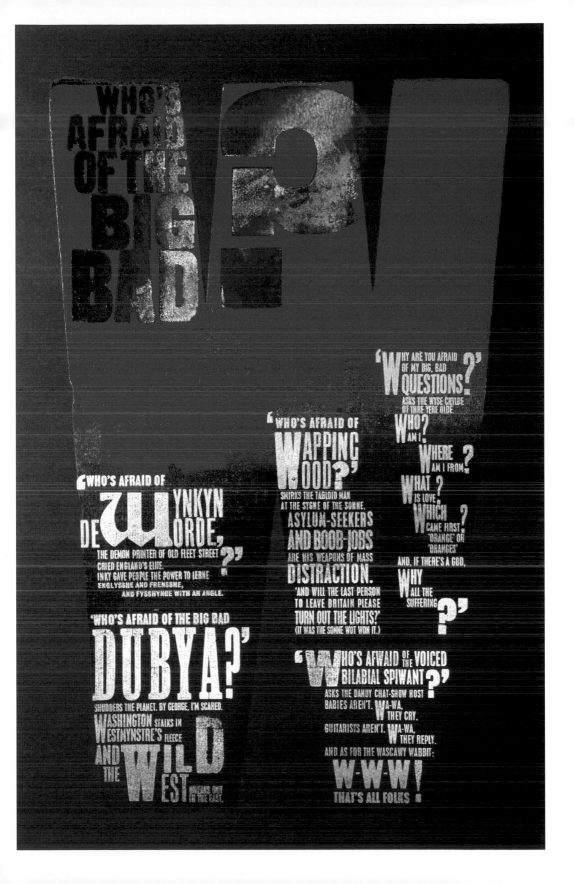

Designer: Alan Kitching
Alan is one of the world's foremost practitioners of letterpress typographic design and printmaking. He is renowned for his expressive use of wood and metal letterforms in creating visuals for commissions and limited editions.

Writer: Dan Radley
Dan has composed political speeches, directed TV commercials, written a musical and appeared naked on posters. You've never heard of him, but he's been parting you from your cash for 20 years. He deserves a slap.

It would be fun to play with the sound and the Englishness of the letter: Jonathan Woss springs to mind.

wavelength **Friday 22 June, Workshop**

Alan's prints and commissions hang from ceiling to floor. Brilliant colour, layered and woven words on view for the Vauxhall Festival.

I've come up with a headline: "Who's afraid of the big, bad W?" (The capital W is typically the widest letterform in a character set.) My plan is to compose a text about fears, rational and irrational, connected with the letter. Example: George W. Bush.

Alan likes the attitude of the line, the way it makes sense of the scale of the poster and the fact it begins and ends with a W.

whimsy **Tuesday 26 June, Florence Street, Islington**

I make a start on verbally embroidering our big, bad W. I've recently rediscovered nonsense verse and I'm feeling inspired by some of the more cautionary rhymes. According to Quentin Blake, it's the apparent decorum of nonsense rhymes that makes them so effective. Spike Milligan said: "Nonsense is taking an absurdity to the point where the reader laughs but doesn't know why. It's wreaking havoc with the English language."

workout **Monday 5 July, Workshop**

I've drafted a number of verses. The stanzas have a disconnected nonsense feel but the underlying themes are dark: for instance, contrasting Wynkyn de Worde, the father of Fleet Street, with modern-day press manipulation.

Alan: After the initial dual V idea I experimented with stencil forms. Now I am working with a wood letter W in a multi-repeat pattern, using small-scale maquettes and a neutral palette of greys and blues to reveal the zigzag shapes within the W letter form.

Wynkyn de Worde **Friday 9 July, British Library**

Dan: The British Library is not my natural domain. Much as I enjoy the detective work, the academic pace frustrates me. On the plus side, the more I find out about the prolific Wynkyn de Worde, the more I like him.

Bibliography
Thanks to the British Library.
Shelf marks in bold.

Berners, Dame Juliana, *A treatise of fysshynge with an angle,* Wynkyn de Worde, 1496 **qL64/1844**

Blake, Quentin (selected by), *The Puffin Book of Nonsense Verse,* Puffin, 1994

Duncan, *The Boar's Head Carol from Wynkyn de Worde's Christmasse Carolles,* 1521 **G.517.y.(1.)**

Firmage, Richard A. *The Alphabet Abecedarium,* Boston: David R. Godine, 1993

Gessler, *A lytell treatyse for to lerne Englysshe and Frensshe,* Wynkyn de Worde **12986.r.11**

Grimm, Jakob and Wilhelm Grimm, *Kinder und Hausmarchen,* 1821 **1551/452**

Halliwell-Phillips, James Orchard, *Popular Rhymes and Nursery Tales of England,* 1843 **X.981/1652**

Heller, Steven, "The meaning of type," *Eye* magazine, volume 50

Lydgate, *A lytell treatise of the horse, the sheep and the ghoos,* Wynkyn de Worde, 1499 **12207.n.35/7**

Man, John, *Alpha Beta. How our alphabet shaped the western world,* Headline, 2000

Moran, James, *Wynkyn de Worde, Father of Fleet Street,* 1976 **2708.aa.62**

Patten, Brian (editor), *The Puffin Book of Utterly Brilliant Poetry,* Puffin, 1999

Rohnell, Ann and Frank Churchill, *Who's Afraid of the Big, Bad Wolf?,* Walt Disney, 1933

Sacks, David, *The Alphabet,* Hutchinson, 2003

Stonehill, Gerald, letter to *The Times,* 3 June 2004

Thompson, Phillip & Peter Davenport, *The Dictionary of Visual Language,* Penguin, 1980

Wynkyn de Worde Society, *A short account of the life and work of Wynkyn de Worde* **C.102.h.19**

My favourite of his published treatises, "Here is a good boke to lern speke frensshe...," turns out to be a kind of Tudor lesson in Franglais.

w-turn **Monday 12 July, phone**

Dan: It's creative tennis. Each ball that's returned changes the course of the rally.

Alan: I've returned to the idea of a single bold W that incorporates Dan's headline and text. I'm still working on producing a 6ft high final piece but the cardboard sheet may not serve the colours well, so I've called paper expert John Purcell for advice.

wait! **Friday 16 July, diary deadline day**

Dan: There are production decisions to be made that will fundamentally affect the outcome of the poster. We ask the publisher to be patient with us.

whittling **Tuesday 20 July, Workshop**

Alan: Purcell Paper delivered an 8ft x 4ft white 5mm Gator Board, and weekend experiments with the 100-line wood letter W, printed in colours and varnishes to enhance the wide and wicked nature of our letter, worked well. But book deadlines may dictate working letterpress in a smaller format and digitally enlarging for the final large-scale exhibit.

My partner Celia and I review the situation and whittle diary words and creative plans to try to meet restrictions and time frames but still exhibit a full-scale hand-printed poster in September. Dan arrives and approves of a possibly eccentric solution...

Dan: This diary was meant to be about the making of a poster. But so far most of the making has happened in our heads. We've built up, eliminated, associated, generalized, verbalized, visualized, defined, manipulated, adapted, combined, separated, repeated, unified, abstracted, expanded, reduced, exaggerated and understated.

And now we're ready to begin.

Thomas Manss + Mike Reed

X stories

I

Thomas said it first: "There's no brief." We were struggling because we had no message to convey. No problem to solve. Just "Do a poster about your letter." Complete creative freedom sounds nice, but it's a roundabout without signposts: if you can go in any direction you want, how do you know which is the right one?

II

X is a brimming banquet of a letter: you tuck in greedily. Then you realize you can never eat it all. We started to get rather queasy, discovering ever more meanings and connections (or connexions).

So we decided to focus on just one or two aspects of X. But that seemed to highlight everything we'd left out. It was like tidying one corner of a room: instead of making the corner look tidy, you just draw attention to the mess around it.

III

Thomas came to the initial meeting with lots of words: quotations, the dictionary. Mike turned up with a couple of entirely graphic ideas. It was a good start: from then on, we didn't worry about who was words and who was pictures.

IV

Mike began by emailing 50 contacts for their thoughts on X. The enthusiastic response was telling: X was fun to think about in a way that G or L probably weren't. The most popular associations were predictable: "X marks the spot," "a kiss," "X-rated." But there was much more: tau crosses, runic symbols, the swastika; da Vinci and Coleridge; cartoon eyes after a whack on the head. One American contact told of her football-hero grandfather: as a girl she thought his middle initial, X, was there to show he'd died. (In fact, his name was Xavier.) Even now, she connects X with absence and loss.

V

Neither of us quite wanted to take the lead. Some of this seemed to come from a shared sense that the other's discipline held the key. Mike thought pictures could speak the thousands of potential words about X; Thomas expected such a verbal conundrum to have a verbal solution. Whatever the reason, it was good news: ego took a back seat to collaboration.

Designer: Thomas Manss
"Where else can one find such impeccable Englishness in a German designer who lives and works in London and Berlin, and manages to possess the virtues of both cultures without the vices?"
Mark Adams, Vitsoe

Writer: Mike Reed
Thirty-five words? An eleven-year career in 35 words? I'm an experienced creative director! I've co-founded my own company! I work with international corporations! And you give me 35 words? All right, here goes – oh, bugger.

VI

When Thomas went looking for X in the visible world, he found it everywhere: in paving stones and cross-beams; telephone wires and twists of pasta; open scissors and manhole covers; tiles and tap handles; wheels and window frames. An excess of Xs.

VII

Early on, struggling to focus our thinking, we made a decision. We didn't want to take ourselves too seriously. We wanted to create what others have called "a smile in the mind." Is that what we've done? We're not quite sure.

VIII

X is hardly a letter at all. It's really just a way of representing combinations of other letters. For egzample, when relaksing in ekzotic lukzhury.

So we imagined the final letters of the alphabet printed so huge that most were heavily cropped. But between W and Y – a gap. Maybe a little paragraph saying… what? X is invisible, because…? It felt rather thin.

We even wondered about an entirely blank canvas, with the faint X-shaped shadow of the frame showing through. A cryptic title card beside it. Nah: cop-out.

Thomas found Ambrose Bierce's *Devil's Dictionary*: "X…, being a needless letter, has an added invincibility to the attacks of the spelling reformers." Perhaps X could be an invincible superhero, demonstrating his powers in a Marvel comic strip. The panels would be arranged so that from a distance, a distinct X-shape would be formed by the mosaic of the strip. OK, but by the end of *July*?

IX

Our first meetings were lengthy, and fairly quiet. The later ones were shorter, and more vocal. We preferred the later ones.

X

An antiques expert, sifting through a long-neglected attic, spots something in the shadows. Something half-obscured by mouldering volumes of *Reader's Digest* and a broken ping-pong table. He can't quite make it out, but there's something about it. Something indefinable, but compelling.

Carried to the window, it looks familiar. A little knot forms in his guts: he might just have something here. Some judicious spit and polish reveals a pattern. He turns it in the speckled light, inverts it. Rubs at the base with his sleeve. And takes a sharp breath, seeing the maker's mark appear through a decade or two of grime.

I knew it, he grins.

But he didn't really; not at first. He just had a feeling. An educated feeling perhaps, informed by experience and a certain talent. But really just a sensation in the gut.

This is the creative bit. The bit you can't explain, even though it's the bit you really get paid for.

Sometimes, inspiration is a light bulb. *Ping!* The answer appears fully formed. Other times – most of the time – you have to coax it out.

At some point, Thomas came upon a three-dimensional wire-frame drawing of X. Like wire-frame cubes, this X flip-flopped: you saw it one way, then the other. Somehow, that resonated: X has multiple aspects. But there was more here. We played with it. We left it alone. We came back to it. Why? It just felt good.

Maybe we could use type to make the lines of the frame? No: too fiddly.

Instead, Thomas tried filling in the panels with paragraphs. Now we had something.

X the invisible letter: there but not there. A letter composed of stories about itself. One thing from a distance, and many things close up.

That feeling in the gut took shape. The object found in the corner started to gleam. We were on to something. Not Meissen, exactly, nor Chippendale. But something nice. Something that would work.

Did it need some sort of title? It did: something to give it an anchor.

"Ten stories about X," one of us said.

"Yes, that's the thought. But it's not really a headline. It needs..."

"Ten stories..."

And then, almost in unison: *"X stories!"*

Bingo.

Malcolm was Little for 27 years. Then he became X and got a great deal bigger. The roots of that change ran deep. His father Earl Little, a civil rights activist, was killed in 1931, two years after the family home burned down. Both were classed as accidents by the police. Meanwhile, Malcolm's ambitions were brutally crushed: a teacher told him the law was 'no realistic goal for a nigger'. After turning to crime, Malcolm educated himself in prison, copying the entire dictionary longhand. He also discovered the Nation of Islam. He took the name 'X' to represent his family's lost African name, which had been replaced by the 'slave name' Little. Malcolm left the NOI, disillusioned, in 1963. In February 1965, he was gunned down at the Audubon Ballroom, New York. Three NOI men were convicted: Talmadge Hayer, Norman 3X Butler and Thomas 15X Johnson. (NOI Members with the same surnames were given numbers to tell them apart.) But Malcolm X's place in the history of civil rights was already assured.

'X marks the spot' is often associated with *Treasure Island*, but the phrase never appears in the book. Its origin is as deeply buried as pirate gold. Some more modern 'pirates', though, have had reason to fear X. In 1930, a book of photographs, *X Marks the Spot: Chicago Gang Wars in Pictures* exposed gangland brutality. It so horrified Al Capone that he ordered it cleared from the shelves. And in Howard Hawks' 1931 movie *Scarface*, X signifies death: when Boris Karloff is killed in a bowling alley, for instance, a ball scatters all the skittles – a "strike" marked with an X.

In 1984, the Canadian poet and musician Robert Priest wrote a story called *The Man Who Broke Out Of The Letter X*, in which a 'beautiful' man breaks out of the letter X and runs screaming in terror around an unnamed city. He's finally caught in a net and dies, horrified. It is a very, very peculiar story indeed.

During the Middle Ages, illiterates (which was just about everybody) signed their names with the sign of the Cross, then sealed it with a kiss. So x became a kiss.

An X on a beer cask used to mean the ten-shilling duty had been paid. So it became a sign of good quality. Later trademarks used XX or XXX to suggest strength. We still think of X (which replaced the original H for 'Horror' in 1951) as the sign of strong cinematic stuff 20 years after it was replaced by the less emotive 18. Although not all filmmakers have forgotten the advantages of being branded XXX.

X is well known as a sign for the mysterious and unknown. We have *The X-Files*, Brand X, the X Factor and *X-Men*. In algebra, x is the basic symbol for an unknown quantity. Some say this is all René Descartes' fault. He chose Z as his primary unknown, then he worked backwards through Y and X. Legend has it that his printer kept running out of Zs and Ys, but had plenty of Xs. So x became the basic sign of the unknown in Descartes' *Géomotrie*. (Certainly, 19th Century printers had a habit of using x when they ran out of other letters.) Another theory is that the Arabic *shel* (which means 'a thing' or 'something') was translated into Greek as *xei*. Victor Hugo's theory was that 'x signifies crossed swords, combat – who will be the victor? Nobody knows – that is why philosophers used x to signify fate and the mathematicians took it for the unknown'. But that's writers for you. It seems fitting that the origins of X as a symbol of the unknown are themselves a bit of a mystery.

The writer Douglas Coupland is credited with popularising the term 'Generation X' to describe those born in the 1960s and 70s, who drifted into bleak lives and 'McJobs'. Coupland says, 'the whole point is that there never was or will be a definition.' But there is a sensibility. When a fellow named Warren badgered Coupland to produce branded T-shirts, Coupland said: 'Warren, keep your money, because nothing could be less X than wearing a T-shirt saying Generation X.' If you understand why, maybe you understand X.

For the writer of this poster, an Englishman, x provides a measure of his words. [illegible] a standard measurement of any typeface, [illegible] not including 'ascenders' [illegible] of its lowercase letters [illegible] 'descenders'. (This isn't the same as the point size, [illegible]) But as usual, when you think you've found some sort of consistent standard, it vanishes. For the designer of this poster, a German, typefaces are measured by their 'x-height'. Typical.

X has been a proper letter for centuries. The Romans attached the Greek sound [illegible] from *xi* (Ξ) to the Greek letter *chi* (X), previously a 'ch' sound. (This was the first letter of 'Christ', which is why we have 'Xmas'.) In English, unlike other letters, X doesn't have its own sound. As Ben Johnson said, X 'is rather an abbreviation, or way of short writing … than a Letter. For it hath the sound of k and s.' In fact, it has the sounds of many letters. X in zylophone, for example, sounds different to X in ankshious or ekzamine. That makes it, according to Ambrose Bierce, 'a needless letter'. Maybe even an ex-letter?

NEW LIGHT SEES THROUGH FLESH TO BONES! screamed the newspapers. In November 1895, Wilhelm Roentgen discovered a new form of radiation so mysterious he named it after the mathematical unknown: 'x-rays'. Roentgen won the first ever Nobel prize for Physics, while 'bone portrait' studios sprung up everywhere, and a London firm produced 'x-ray-proof' lead underwear. An Iowa farmer even claimed to have used x-rays to transform base metal into gold. But everybody saw straight through that one.

X STORIES

Brian Webb + Margaret Oscar

Margaret's diary

I don't care what people say, it really isn't the same. Writing and providing a writer with direction for their writing are two very different things, and require two very different skill sets. Being a brand manager for verbal identity means I spend much of my time helping writers write. Of course, I'm expected to write too. But I have to be honest and confess that when it comes to the act of writing, I much prefer directing to doing.

Having said that, I'd rather attempt to craft words into a written piece of communication than design something visual involving imagery, and so I took the role of writer in this project. My designer Brian Webb, an astute chap who quickly recognized my reluctance, decided to cut to the chase and pick up the phone to me. I felt much better once we'd spoken. (I remain convinced, however, that designers can smell fear.)

One of the first things Brian asked me was why I chose the letter Y. I chose it because I was looking for a letter that was desperate to misbehave, a consonant that wanted to be a vowel, a letter that also masqueraded as a word, a member of the alphabet that could make several sounds within the English language.

Even within other languages, Y is a chameleon, adopting the shape of other letters in order to belong. I decided it was a bit of an upstart, always trying to be something other than itself, never happy with its station in life. There was even a hint of arrogance about it, in the way it assumed it had a right to behave like this. But as we worked, we dug up some interesting background on my cheeky letter, a history that suddenly made sense of its behaviour.

Y originated from the Greek upsilon, the twentieth letter of the Greek alphabet. It was written as a Y by the Romans after the conquest of Greece, solely to indicate words borrowed from the Greek. It was sometimes known as the letter of Pythagoras because he used the upsilon as the symbol for human life: the stem representing innocence and the two branches, vice and virtue. In the Middle Ages, it was often used to denote the "th" sound, apparent in words such as "ye" for "the." Today, it behaves as a semi-vowel, changing its sound depending on where in a word it sits.

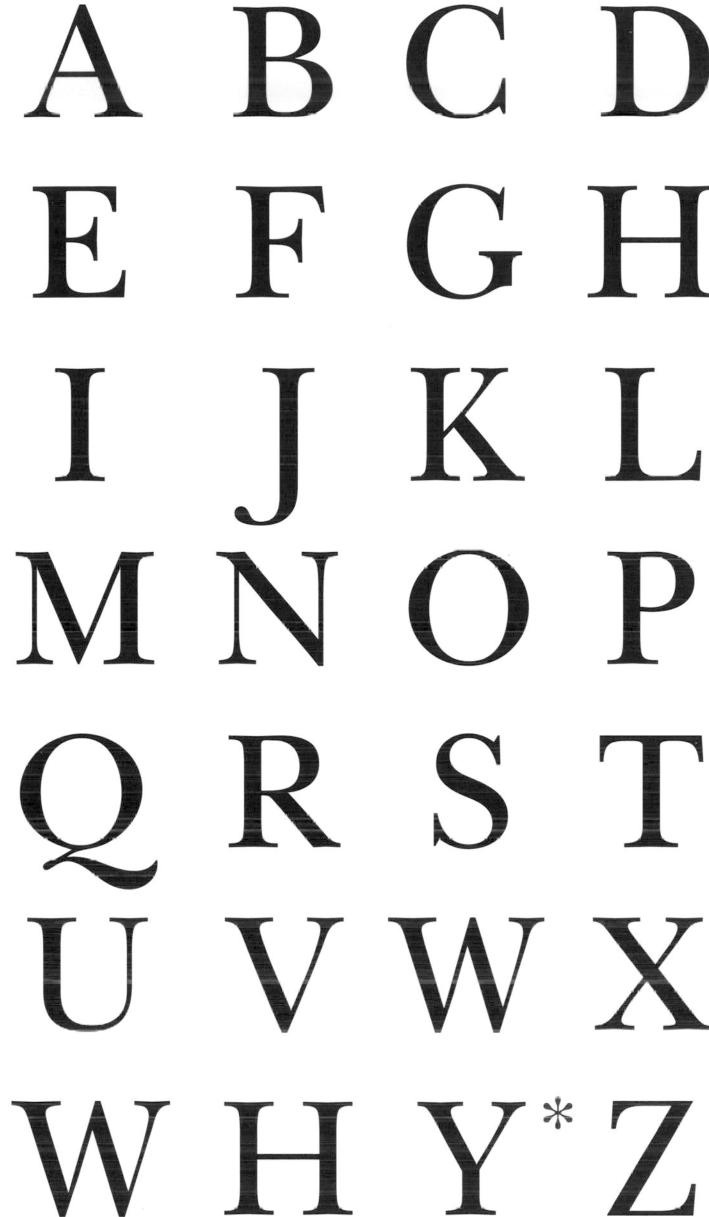

A B C D
E F G H
I J K L
M N O P
Q R S T
U V W X
W H Y* Z

*Y wants to be a vowel, a symbol that is a shy yet happy consonant. The type all letters aspire to be.

Words Margaret Oscar, Design Brian Webb, Type Baskerville

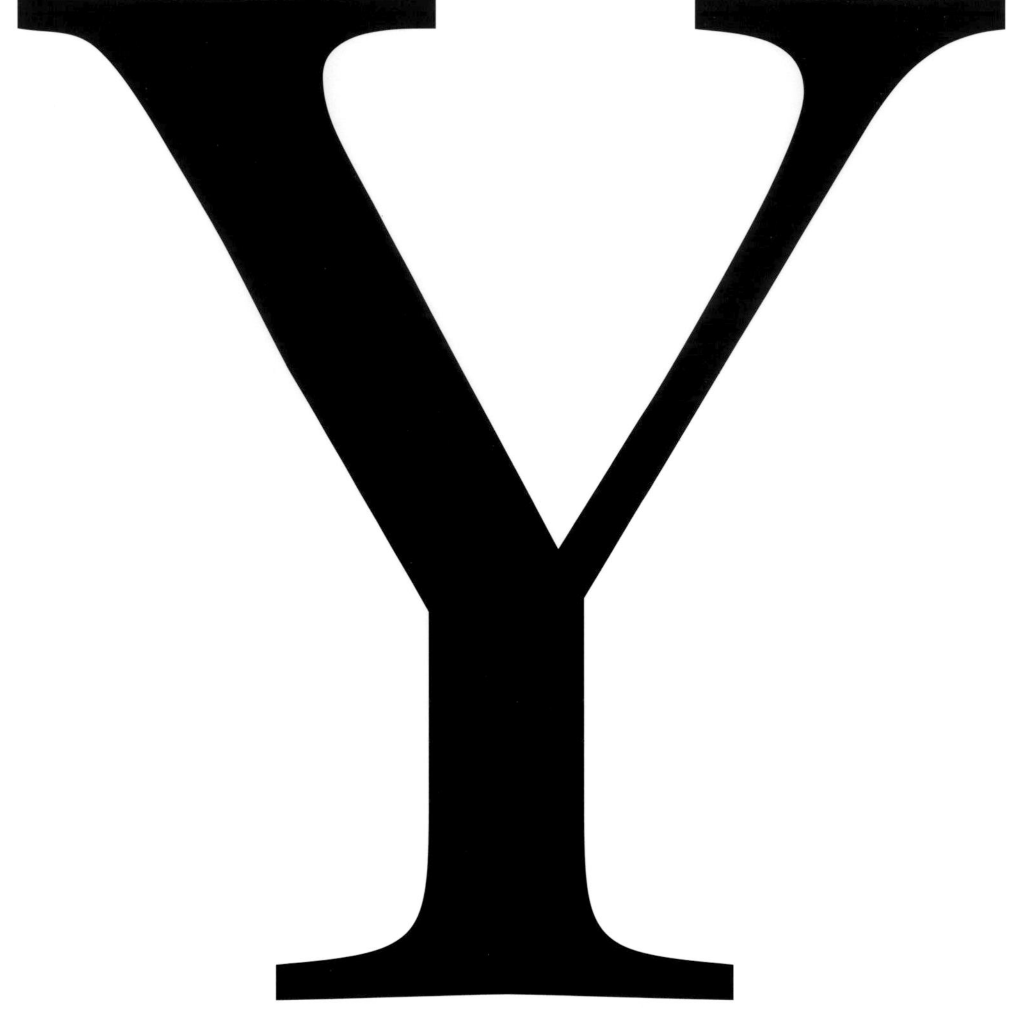

Designer: Brian Webb
Brian Webb co-founded Trickett & Webb in 1971 and in 2003 became designer/director of Webb & Webb. He is currently president of the Chartered Society of Designers and visiting professor at the University of the Arts, London.

Writer: Margaret Oscar
Margaret specializes in expressing the personality of commercial organizations through their written communications. She's blessed with the kind of assertive leadership and friendly manner that makes things happen in business.

What little is known about the history of Y is chequered with accounts of how it was never itself but always a substitute for something else. Even the English dictionary describes it as a symbol used for unknown variables like numbers or people. Is it any wonder that it now tries to play so many roles, says its own name using the sound of another letter and is never satisfied with its position in the alphabet (not first, not last, but always almost)?

We decided that we needed a visual presentation that demonstrated its frustration and demand to be more than a substitute. Something bold and pushy, but not letting Y forget its place in the chain of command. And something that would communicate its attitude and make clear its conviction that it is capable of more than it's allowed. A tall order, so imagine how thrilled I was when Brian decided he wanted to handle the design and leave the writing to me.

After a meeting at the Fine Art Society – a tranquil setting for our flurried production of papers that expressed our exchanged random thoughts and sketches – we went off to our separate parts of the world (Torquay and South London), where I began to articulate our thoughts and he created a visual representation of every raw idea we discussed. The first result was so simple, and so right, that we were both silent for a few moments after we saw it on a wall. Brian was equally pleased with this little rendition of the journey we began together, changing nothing but a spelling mistake.

Zz

Alan Dye + Alastair Creamer

Alan's diary

20 April Received the brief for the 26 Letters poster. First thought: shit! All the luminaries of the design world are in there – and me! Second thought: where are my partners' names? Nick Finney, Ben Stott and myself have been running our design practice for over six years, and almost every project is a collaboration.

Third thought: end of July deadline, loads of time.

Fourth, fifth, and sixth thoughts: Z - Z - Z.

Zax (zaks) [A.-S. seax], n. A slater's hatchet with a sharp point for perforating the slate, a sax.

8 May Arranged a meeting at my studio with Alastair Creamer. Work is hectic at the moment: two designers have left and their replacements are yet to be found. A difficult task considering there are zillions (I'm beginning to think of Z things) of graphic designers pouring out of art colleges.

Zarf (zarf), [Arab.], n. An ornamental cup-shaped holder for a hot coffee-cup.

17 May Alastair bounced into the studio, an enigmatic character full of energy. I'm knackered! There's been a deadline every day now for about three weeks and I can't see an end to it. Needless to say the letter Z has been as distant from my mind as it is from the letter A. Over a coffee we learn a little about each other and discuss our letter. We sketch, chat and pen a meeting in for a couple of weeks' time.

Zoom (zoom) [onomat.], (Aviat.) To turn upwards suddenly at a very sharp angle.

20 May Introductory meeting at the British Library. Led into a lecture theatre where we would supposedly be familiarized with using the British Library's resources. One lady gave a fantastic short talk on the history of Illuminated letterforms. I've been driving past the British Library since its construction in the early 1990s and always wanted to go in, but shamefully have never visited. What a wonderful place.

Zooid (zo'oid), a. Having the nature of an animal, having organic life and motion. n. A more or less independent organism developed by fission or gemmation; a member of a compound organism; an organic body or cell capable of independent motion.

24 May Alastair is full of ideas. There are over 500 places in the world beginning with Z! I've done nothing apart from look up zombies on the internet.

Zimb (zimb) [Arab.] n. A dipterous insect common in Abyssinia resembling the tsetse, and hurtful to cattle.

9 June *Zenmeyang* (Mandarin for howzat)! The Chinese have apparently taken up cricket in a big way. I have an idea: British Library – words – reading – diary – collaboration. Why not create a poster out of our diaries? There are only 135 words beginning

Zingaro (zing'ga ro) [It.], n. (pl. -ri, re) A gipsy.

We've worked together on this project but it was Alan who came up with the two ideas that would literally shape our poster. The first was the decision to cover the page with our writing – diaries, quotes, stories, thoughts from friends, musings – and then out of this 3,000 Odyssey a large, shimmering Z would appear. Initially we thought we could do this purely through alternating the pressure of pencil on paper. But several trials (and one massive false start) later we settled on 3B and 8B Faber-Castell pencils (we refined this down to a 2B). We've done all our work at Alan's studio just off Tottenham Court Road. Come to think of it, I've never seen Alan outside his office! We've listened to lots of music, drunk tea, swapped stories. At times it's seemed effortless, but the reality for both of us was that when we got together we instinctively pushed things aside, shoehorned time in and started talking. Out of that seemingly 'unproductive' time came this perfect marriage of design and content. Yeah, well we would say that wouldn't we! Anyway, Alan's last piece of advice before I start on this properly is: "go easy on your R's", so that's what I'm doing. To begin with I started at the end – with Z. I'd asked for it (the letter that is) [illegible] be written. An intriguing challenge. But where to start? I found myself [illegible] of different [illegible] of pages scanning the dictionary, feeling the increasing weight of responsibility as time passed. Nothing. Zilch. I chased some lost causes: perhaps the highest scoring word in Scrabble would be something like razzmatazz (it isn't and apparently there's only two Zs in a game). Names and faces drifted into my thoughts – Zorro, Zadok, Zidane, Zebedee, Ziggy, Zorba, Zappa, Zhivago and with them came images of Anthony Hopkins in a mask, Nigel Hawthorne in The Madness of George III, Zidane's weird bald patch, Emma Thompson (I'm sure her Dad had something to do with The Magic Roundabout), that ring of make-up on Bowie's forehead, Anthony Quinn dancing against a sublime Grecian backdrop, Frank's goatee and Omar's moustache. I thought of the difference between zed and zee (when was I aware that there was ever a difference?) and also of how my computer keeps American-izing everything by substituting Zs (or zees). What have we got against them anyway? They add a bit of style to a word. Let's face it [illegible] S. In desperation I phoned a friend in Brussels who's a bit of a linguist – did he know of any alphabet or language that didn't use Z? [illegible] a list of my favourite words beginning with Z; those that used a ZZ (this was a great list); words that sounded as if they should start with Z [illegible] xenophobia – now rapidly acquiring a new meaning for me, a fear of the letter Z). But something strange was happening. Z is a letter with so much associated energy – zap, zing, zeal, zillions, zoom, zest, zenith, zealot, zany, zip and yet, at the same time it was draining me. I felt zonked. [illegible] one night, watching the telly distracted, my glance zeroed in on the atlas we keep tucked away on a low shelf, out of the way. I opened it at the index in the back under Z and there was my answer, in fact hundreds of them: Zagazig (Egypt), Zagreb, Zaire, Zambeze, Zanesville (USA), Z[illegible], Zermatt, Zhangzhou and Zibo (China), Zimbabwe, Ziz (Morocco), Zongo (Zaire), Zorzor (Liberia), Zouch (Nottinghamshire – I just thought [illegible]), Zug, Zurich and Zygi (in Cyprus – the last place in my atlas). These were names that conjured up places, people, holidays, cultures [illegible] and dreams. And then, of course, there was the most famous place of all beginning with Z – Zverinogolovskoye – that renowned Russian hideaway [illegible] over 500 of them compared to only 100 or so words in the dictionary. Z firmly belonged on the pages of an atlas. It was more suited to representing [illegible] words. So I started thinking about Z in terms of travel, as a concept rather than a letter – a fixed chiselled shape. Suddenly, it became something [illegible] the line, a possible destination, even a starting point, a pause in your journey, a watering hole en route. It could be the [illegible] but whatever it stands for, it is elusive, exotic, just out of reach, at the ends of the earth, the back of beyond, somewhere over the rainbow [illegible] point you never knew existed (just try turning an N on its side). But it is there – like Xanadu, Utopia, Platform 9¾ [illegible] as well as your desired destination from which you turn. Z is like a postcard that has no place [illegible] a direction half remembered, a restaurant someone raved about but never gave you the exact [illegible] through distortion, the road that seems to lead nowhere. Z is like an eclipse behind a cloud. Alan' [illegible] on Charlotte Street, Soho. Carried on the discussion about her local swimming pool. A [illegible] about doing some exercise and swimming seems to be the best bet. Speedo [illegible] (I was with Ben, one of my two partners from NB: Studio at the time) be interested in creating a poster [illegible] Zabra (za'bra) [Sp] n. A small sailing vessel formerly used on the coasts of the Iberian Peninsula. May 13th: [illegible] are on there – and me! Second thought: where are my two partners names? Nick Finney, Ben Stott [illegible] is a collaboration. Third thought: end of July deadline [illegible] Zax (zaks) [A-S seax] n. A slater's hatchet with a sharp point for perforating the slate [illegible] Cramer, my 'Z' partner. I email back and arrange a meeting at my studio. Work is hectic at the moment [illegible] A difficult task considering there are zillions (I'm beginning to think of Z things) [illegible] Zarf (zarf) [Arab] n. An ornamental cup shaped holder for a hot coffee cup. May 17th: Alastair [illegible] There's been a presentation or deadline every day now for about [illegible] the letter Z has been as distant from my mind as it is from the letter A. Over a tea we heard a little about each other [illegible] couple of weeks time. Zoom (zoom) [onomat.], (Aviat.) To turn upwards suddenly at a very sharp angle. May 20th: [illegible] a few familiar faces and was led into a lecture theatre where we supposedly would [illegible] I didn't have a bloody clue what the two ladies were talking about. [illegible] I've been driving past the British Library since its construction [illegible] What a wonderful place. Picked up my reader card and spent a couple of hours exploring the library [illegible] May 24th: Alastair has written loads and is full of ideas. There are over 500 places in the world beginning with Z. [illegible] We arrange another meeting. Zimb (zimb) [Arab] n. A dipterous insect common in Abyssinia [illegible] 'Zinvelyang' Mandarin for 'Howzat' The Chinese have apparently taken up cricket [illegible] collaboration. Why not create a poster out of our diaries? There are only 135 words beginning with Z [illegible] Alastair has had so many thoughts and great ideas about Z, why not express them all? Let's celebrate our letter. [illegible] the poster to be a collaboration in its execution as much as the content. We will fill a sheet of paper [illegible] with our thoughts, in our handwriting, using a pencil. I will map out a capital Z in the middle [illegible] with the 3B pencil. The result – I don't know until we try it, but I think it will work. Zooid (zo'oid) a [illegible] out motion. n. A more or less independent organism developed by fission or gemmation [illegible] of independent motion. July 15th: Work has quietened down a little. I order some large paper [illegible] and buy a gaggle of soft pencils. I like the idea that this poster has become a physical challenge. I'm ignoring [illegible] everything that I use in my general graphic design work: grids, typefaces, colours, inks, embossing, typesetting, images and printers [illegible] sheet and Alastair and I start writing and experimenting with HB pencils. It works!!! Alastair will plan the order and structure [illegible] responsible for most of the words but I will still have to find at least 1,500 words about Z!!! Lazy or just good at delegation. [illegible] and receive some bizarre and great thoughts on their interpretation of Z. It all adds to the texture and makes [illegible] looking for that swimming pool! Zythum (zi'thum) [Gr zuthos], n. A malt beverage used in Ancient Egypt. Alastair's diary continues on from [illegible] July: My day starts with frantic phone calls to Australia after I hear my son Ollie has been knocked out snowboarding and helicoptered off the mountain (he's fine). My eyes prick as I speak to him in the emergency ward. I know the day is going to conclude with a difficult meeting. Someone's been rubbed up the wrong way! In the middle of all this is the oasis that is Alan and our Z poster. Today of all days I need him to be fun, generous, present [illegible] all these things despite the fact that he has a thumping, walloping hangover. Big party last night and can't seem to shift it despite large doses [illegible] our deadline for these diaries. Not so, says Alan. Saw the woman who's in charge of these at the party and she said Monday's fine. We've got a reprieve. The man's a genius, sober and drunk. The hangover's worth it just for this alone. On the ping pong table which serves as our work top our gigantic poster is laid out. Alan has drawn 100 lines across it. It is pristine, prepared, poised. First we need to trial the idea. Alan's had a first stab so I now write the 30 lines of my script on to another huge piece of paper alternating soft and hard pencils. After ten lines I get into a rhythm. My handwriting seems [illegible] it still takes an hour. When I stick the results on the wall the whole office get up as one to come and look. They like it in a quiet way (most of them are [illegible] too). Alan is the centre of need. He starts with me and then gets pulled off on a job someone else wants him on the phone. He's seeing a designer later and needs to schedule that and then there's something he has to sort out for his girlfriend ('she'll kill me if I don't make this call' – this is the famous girlfriend who's been to Zanzibar – an early Z connection). Someone's going to M&S. He asks them to get him a fruit juice and a blood transfusion. In between all this we haggle over margins. I'm concerned that as the lines are so long, if somebody (you, for instance) actually wants to read our ramblings they'll never find their way to the start of the next line (did you manage it?). This doesn't worry Alan. He likes the writing to the edge of the page. In the end I think I gain an inch each side. And this is one of my real weaknesses – tweaking, shaping someone's else's ideas. The amateur designer in me coming out. I do this all the time at work (I've done it ever since I can remember) and it drives designers mad. Another example: Alan had come across a typeface called Ziggurat. To me, it's blindingly obvious we've got to use it. It's squat, producing a square Z that seems to fold back on itself. It's just meant to be because it starts with a Z. Alan, in his wisdom, wants something cleaner, simpler. And, of course, he's right. The Z he's picked is the bare minimum a Z needs to be – across, down, across. The end result will be beautiful. Saturday 17th July: I now realize why this diary was destined to be late. In this morning's Guardian there's a piece about how Heinz has put the Z back into Beanz. Beanz Meanz Heinz was dreamed up in a London pub by Maurice Drake in 1967. It was voted best slogan of all time in 2000 and now, at last, beans has the spelling it deserves. English teachers everywhere will be cursing Heinz as they red-line increased mis-spellings until eventually they give up and admit defeat. Zs are making a comeback. They're in fashion. I'm working on the most important, pivotal, letter at the moment of its coup. The end. Here are a few messages of support from some of Alan's friends and colleagues. From: David Fowle. Re: Z. Alan Dye, entrepreneur extraordinaire and full-time shark asked me to come up with some copy for a meaningful poster which features the letter Z. Sadly, the poster is quite large and needs copious amounts of copy. So how do I fill the space? Should I write things like, 'Zidane he is ze best football player in ze world'. Or, is the plural of Kangaroo Kangarooz? There's also that song 'Zippedy something or other' where the guy's walking along with animated blue birds fluttering around his head. No, I thought. That's a load of old cobblers. And then, suddenly, it hit me like a wet haddock around the chops. A few months ago, Alan started designing a business card for me on the vague promise of a free meal purchased by me at no fixed time in the unforeseeable future. I now realise this was (there you go, I haven't forgotten) a severe error on my behalf. You don't get anything for free in this life anyway. My fault for being a cheapskate I suppose. As a result Alan has blackmailed me into writing this bit of copy, by saying things like, 'F***ing hell Fowlee, I'm designing all your corporate identity s***. The least you can do is write a bit of copy'. Fair enough, I totally agree I said. Several months on however, Alan has his copy while I'm still waiting for my business card. Lazzzzzzzzzzzzzzzzzzzzzzzzzzzzzzzzzzzzy old bastard.

Alastair Cramer   Alan Dye

Designer: Alan Dye
While at Pentagram I met my two future partners, Nick Finney and Ben Stott. Together we started NB:Studio, a multi-disciplinary design company with a broad range of clients from furniture makers and galleries to publishers and cosmetic companies. We believe in the importance of a good idea.

Writer: Alastair Creamer
I trained as a musician and have spent my life running arts organizations. I've created most of the jobs I've done, including my current one which brings together business and the arts.

with Z in the *Concise Oxford Dictionary* (1988); Alastair has had so many great ideas about Z, why not express them all? Let's celebrate our letter. I run the idea past Alastair; he likes it.

We want the poster to be a collaboration in its execution as much as its content. We will fill a sheet of paper (1,040mm wide x 1,555mm high, 4 sheet – a sense of scale is important) with our thoughts, in our handwriting, using a pencil. I will map out a capital Z in the middle and when we cross it we will press harder with the 3B pencil. The result? I don't know until we try it, but I think it will work.

16 July I order some large paper (thank you Justin at Fenner Paper) and buy a gaggle of soft pencils. I like the idea that this poster has become a physical challenge. I'm ignoring my daily tool, the computer, and everything I use in my general graphic design work: grids, typefaces, colours, inks, embossing, typesetting, images and printers. I map out a test sheet and Alastair and I start writing and experimenting with HB pencils. It works! Alastair will plan the order and structure of the text and will be responsible for most of the words, but I will still have to find at least 1,500 words about Z.

Zythum (zi'thum,) [Gr.zuthos], n. A malt beverage used in Ancient Egypt.

Lazy or good at delegation, I email a number of friends and clients a tiny brief and receive some bizarre interpretations of Z. They all add to the texture and make funny and interesting reading.

Alastair's diary (last two days)

16 July My day starts with frantic phone calls to Australia after I hear my son has been knocked out snowboarding and helicoptered from the mountain. He's fine. My eyes prick as I speak to him in the emergency ward. And then I know the day is going to conclude with a difficult meeting. Someone's been rubbed up the wrong way. In the middle of all this is the oasis that is Alan. Today of all days I need him to be fun, generous, present. And he is all these things even though he has a thumping hangover.

On the ping-pong table our gigantic poster is laid out. Alan has drawn 100 lines across it. It is pristine, prepared, poised. First we need to trial the idea. Alan's had a first stab so I now write the 30 lines of my script onto another huge piece of paper alternating soft and hard pencils.

After ten lines I get into a rhythm. My handwriting relaxes. It still takes an hour.

Alan is the centre of need. He starts with me and is then required on a job. Someone else wants him on the phone. He's seeing a designer later and needs to schedule that and then there's something he has to sort out for his girlfriend. In between all this we haggle over margins. I'm concerned that the lines are so long that if somebody actually wants to read our ramblings they'll never find their way to the start of the next line. This doesn't worry Alan. He likes the writing going to the edge of the page. In the end I think I gain an inch each side.

And this is one of my real weaknesses – tweaking, shaping. The amateur designer in me coming out. I do this all the time at work and it drives designers mad. Another example: Alan had come across a typeface called Ziggurat. To me, it's blindingly obvious we've got to use it. It's squat, producing a square Z that seems to fold back on it-self. It's meant to be because it starts with a Z. Alan wants something cleaner, simpler. He's right. The Z he's picked is the bare minimum a Z needs to be – across, down, across.

The end result will be beautiful.

17 July I now realize why this diary had to be late. In this morning's *Guardian* there's a piece about how Heinz has put the Z back into Beanz. Beanz Meanz Heinz was dreamed up in a London pub by Maurice Drake in 1967. It was voted best slogan of all time in 2000, and now at last beans has the spelling it deserves. English teachers everywhere will be cursing Heinz as they red-line multiplying misspellings until eventually they admit defeat. Zs are making a comeback. Z is going to turn English on its head. I've arrived at last at my meaning. I'm working on the most important, pivotal letter at the very moment of its coup.

About ISTD

The International Society of Typographic Designers (ISTD) is the only authoritative international body for typography. Its aim is to inform and inspire typographers, graphic designers, writers and educators engaged in the field of visual communication. It unites those who are passionate about type and typography, promoting awareness of the subject through widespread activities including lectures and exhibitions, as well as an annual Student Assessment Scheme and biennial professional awards.

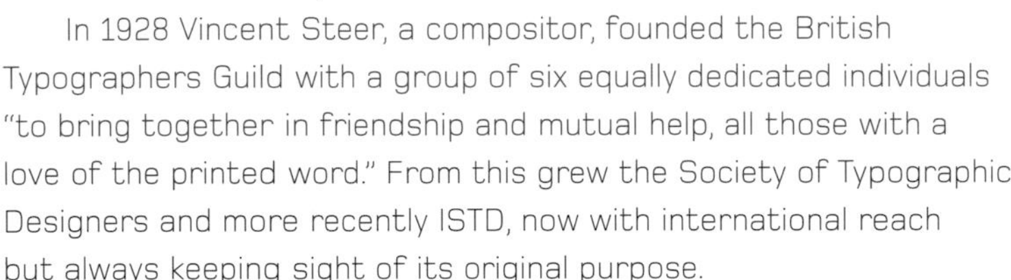

In 1928 Vincent Steer, a compositor, founded the British Typographers Guild with a group of six equally dedicated individuals "to bring together in friendship and mutual help, all those with a love of the printed word." From this grew the Society of Typographic Designers and more recently ISTD, now with international reach but always keeping sight of its original purpose.

Membership of the Society confers professional status on a designer. Its affix means that a member has reached a high standard of design and has agreed to the ISTD's code of ethics.

There are four categories of ISTD membership: Honorary Fellowship (Hon FISTD), Fellowship (FISTD), Membership (MISTD) and Corporate Membership, through which design organizations, agencies and other related institutions support the Society.

Membership is offered to students successfully completing the Society's annual Student Assessment Scheme. Initiated in 1977, the scheme now runs in four countries. It brings together members from practice and education to assess the work of prospective young members. The growing digital archive of students' work is a valuable record of contemporary typographic design at college level, and has become an important resource for tutors.

Members receive *TypoGraphic*, the ISTD's journal and forum for constructive critical debate about typography and graphic communication, featuring contributions from leading designers and educators. First published in 1971, *TypoGraphic* has chronicled three dynamic decades of typographic development, winning awards for its design and praise for its content.

ISTD publishes a range of books and catalogues arising from its activities. For further information and membership applications visit the Society's website *www.istd.org.uk* or email info@istd.org.uk.

About 26

Writing is part of everyday life. We experience it in the scripted announcements on a station platform, a letter from our local authority or the annual report of a company we trust. Despite its ubiquity, writing is often rejected by readers because it is boring, confusing or irrelevant. What a waste of effort!

26 is a not-for-profit association of professional writers, language specialists and anyone else who cares about writing and language. We called ourselves 26 after the number of letters in the alphabet – the DNA of language. After meeting informally to discuss our experiences, we decided to turn 26 into a group dedicated to improving the use of writing in business and everyday life.

When we launched 26 in September 2003, we thought it would take a few years to grow to twenty-six people. After one year we have more than 200 paid-up members and a further 250 people on our mailing list.

Our members come from all sorts of areas in business and life. We are entrepreneurs, writers, photographers, editors, designers, poets, lawyers, branding consultants, scriptwriters, broadcasters, advertising creative directors, managers, retailers, publishers, marketing directors and, yes, even an accountant.

We believe that improving the quality of writing in business is not just about inspiring companies to commission great writers. Many employees spend much of their day working with words, writing emails, letters, reports, briefs and presentations, as well as talking to customers and colleagues. Helping employees to develop better language skills can improve the way a company relates to people. It's also a very accessible (and inexpensive) way to develop greater creativity and better communication within the workplace.

Words add so much to our lives. Good writing can excite, challenge, intrigue, move, enlighten and entertain us. Writing can also be a satisfying, enjoyable and effective way to express our ideas at work. Lots of great people seem to share this view. 26 is here to bring them together, and spread the word.

www.26.org.uk

About the British Library

The British Library houses the world's knowledge, and represents an inspirational resource for the creative industries. Its unrivalled collections provide fertile ground for creative practitioners in every medium to develop work that engages new audiences.

With over 150 million separate items, the British Library is one of the top three libraries in the world. It is the UK's national library and the world's leading resource for scholarship, research and innovation. Its collection covers every age of written civilization, every written language and every aspect of human thought. The material it holds ranges from ancient Chinese oracle bones to technical reports about the latest scientific discoveries and today's newspapers.

Users have access to the library's collection in its Reading Rooms and via its global document supply services, which supply over 15,000 documents per day to 20,000 customers in 111 countries. Information on the collection and services is available on the British Library website at *www.bl.uk*.

About the London Design Festival

The London Design Festival celebrates and promotes London as the creative capital of the world, and the gateway to the UK's world-class creative community. The Festival brings together over sixty organizations involved in the creative industries with over seventy events across the capital during a two-week period in September each year.

We work with individuals and partner organizations around London to stage events and activities all over town. These events are eclectic – including seminars and exhibitions, film screenings, competitions and awards and even the odd party – and bring together people with a range of interests from lifestyle to urban regeneration. The Festival aims to represent every form of pioneering design, from architecture to advertising, new media to product design, graphic design to fashion.

It's an inclusive Festival, with an emphasis on new talent through links with design education and young entrepreneurs, as well as the more established organizations such as professional membership bodies, local and national government departments, creative businesses, museums and galleries.

We encourage and facilitate collaboration across different design sectors and organizations – this project with ISTD, 26 and the British Library is one very successful and rewarding example, showing just what can happen when you put creative minds together.

To find out more, please visit *www.londondesignfestival.com.*

Designers' contact details

Aa
Roger Fawcett-Tang
Struktur Design Limited
24 Citybridge House
235–245 Goswell Road
London
EC1V 7JD

T: +44 (0)20 7837 2535
info@struktur.co.uk
www.struktur-design.com

Bb
Christine Fent
Christine Fent Design
110 Foundling Court
Brunswick Centre
Marchmont Street
London
WC1N 1AN

T: +44 (0)20 7837 1643
F: +44 (0)20 7278 9433
cf@christinefentdesign.com
www.christinefentdesign.com

Cc
Morag Myerscough
Studio Myerscough
30D Great Sutton Street
London
EC1V 0DS

T: +44 (0)20 7689 0808
F: +44 (0)20 7689 0909
morag@studiomyerscough.co.uk
www.studiomyerscough.com

Dd
David Quay
David Quay Design
Pieter Jacobszstraat 33
Amsterdam 1012 HL
The Netherlands

T: +31 (0)20 528 6050
d.quay@planet.nl
www.foundrytypes.co.uk

Ee
Lucienne Roberts
sans+baum
Third floor
3 Westland Place
London
N1 7LP

T: +44 (0)20 7490 8880
sans@dircon.co.uk

Ff
Ben Parker & Paul Austin
MadeThought
Studio 6
Jamaica Wharf
2 Shad Thames
London
SE1 2YU

T: +44 (0)20 7378 0099
F: +44 (0)20 7378 0173
info@madethought.com
www.madethought.com

Gg
Nick Bell
5.06 Tea Building
5–13 Bethnal Green Road
London
E1 6LA

T: +44 (0)7950 269292
nickbelldesign@easynet.co.uk

Hh
Andrew Monk
andrew.monk@nokia.com

Ii
Derek Birdsall
Omnific
T: +44 (0)20 7359 1201

Jj
Christian Altmann
& Stuart Youngs
CDT Design Limited
21 Brownlow Mews
London
WC1N 2LG

T: +44 (0)20 7539 7706
F: +44 (0)20 7242 1174
christian@cdt-design.co.uk
stuart@cdt-design.co.uk
www.cdt-design.co.uk

Kk
Marksteen Adamson
ArthurSteenAdamson
The Summit
2 Castle Hill Terrace
Maidenhead
Berkshire
SL6 4JP

T: +44 (0)1628 770360
F: +44 (0)1628 780799
me@marksteen.com
www.asaemail.com

Ll
Tom Green
Grade Design Consultants
Sarsons Brewery Works
5 Maltings Place
169 Tower Bridge Road
London
SE1 3NA

T: +44 (0)20 7403 1984
F: +44 (0)20 7015 9032
tom@gradedesign.com
www.gradedesign.com

Mm
Angus Hyland
Pentagram Design
11 Needham Road
London
W11 2RP

T: +44 (0)20 7229 3477
hyland@pentagram.co.uk
www.pentagram.com

Nn
Gilmar Wendt
SAS
6 Salem Road
London
W2 4BU

T: +44 (0)20 7243 3232
F: +44 (0)20 7243 3216
gwendt@sasdesign.co.uk
www.sasdesign.co.uk

Oo
Rick Sellars
35a Glebe Road
Crouch End
London
N8 7DA

T: +44 (0)7736 857614
rick@northdesign.co.uk

Pp
Bryan Edmondson
SEA Design
70 St John Street
London
EC1M 4DT

T: +44 (0)20 7566 3100
F: +44 (0)20 7566 3101
bryan@seadesign.co.uk
www.seadesign.co.uk

Qq
Alan Fletcher
12 Pembridge Mews
London
W11 3EQ

T: +44 (0)20 7229 7095
F: +44 (0)20 7229 8120
alan@afletcher.co.uk

Rr
Michael Johnson
johnson banks
Crescent Works
Crescent Lane
London
SW4 9RW

T: +44 (0)20 7587 6400
F: +44 (0)20 7587 6411
michael@johnsonbanks.co.uk
www.johnsonbanks.co.uk

Ss
Erik Spiekermann
United Designers Network
Motzstrasse 59
10777 Berlin
Germany

T: +49 30 212 80 80
F: +49 30 212 80 810
erik@uniteddesigners.com
www.uniteddesigners.com

Tt
Henrik Kubel
A2-GRAPHICS/SW/HK
Unit G3
35-40 Charlotte Road
London
EC2A 3PD

T: +44 (0)20 7739 4249
henrik@a2-graphics.co.uk

Uu
Peter Dawson
Grade Design Consultants
Sarsons Brewery Works
5 Maltings Place
169 Tower Bridge Road
London
SE1 3NA

T: +44 (0)20 7403 1984
F: +44 (0)20 7015 9032
peter@gradedesign.com
www.gradedesign.com

Vv
Lila Szagun
15 Cliffview Road
London
SE13 7DB

T: +44 (0)7990 630707
lilaszagun@yahoo.co.uk
www.lilaszagun.co.uk

Ww
Alan Kitching
The Typography Workshop
19 Cleaver Street
London
SE11 4DP

T: +44 (0)20 7091 0772
F: +44 (0)20 7820 8098

Xx
Thomas Manss
Thomas Manss & Company
3 Nile Street
London
N1 7LX

T: +44 (0)20 7251 7777
F: +44 (0)20 7251 7778
thomas@manss.com
www.manss.com

Yy
Brian Webb
Webb & Webb Design
16H Perseverance Works
38 Kingsland Road
London
E2 8DD

T: +44 (0)20 7739 7895
F: +44 (0)20 7729 0500
design@webbandwebb.co.uk
www.webbandwebb.co.uk

Zz
Alan Dye
NB:Studio
24 Store Street
London
WC1E 7BA

T: +44(0)20 7580 9195
F: +44(0)20 7580 9196
a.dye@nbstudio.co.uk
www.nbstudio.co.uk

Writers' contact details

Aa
Sean Lewis
Finisterre
Shiva Building
The Tanneries
Bermondsey Street
London
SE1 3XH

T: +44 (0)20 7357 9333
F: +44 (0)20 7357 9383
sean@finisterre.co.uk
www.finisterre.co.uk

Bb
Mark Fiddes
Euro RSCG London
Cupola House
15 Alfred Place
London
WC1E 7EB

T: +44 (0)20 7257 6002
F: +44 (0)20 7467 9282
mark.fiddes@eurorscg.com
www.eurorscg.co.uk

Cc
Charlotte Rawlins
charlotte.rawlins@ntlworld.com

Dd
Gordon Kerr
Vox Marketing Limited
20 Marlborough Close
Fleet
Hampshire
GU51 3HY

T: +44 (0)1252 620405
M: +44 (0)7789 992832
F: +44 (0)1252 620405
gordon@voxgo.f2s.com

Ee
Tom Lynham
International Wordstorming
19 Nichols Court
Cremer Street
London
E2 8HR

T: +44 (0)7779 260450
F: +44 (0)20 7012 1119
tlynham@dircon.co.uk
www.26.org.uk

Ff
Laura Forman
Interbrand
85 Strand
London
WC2R 0DW

T: +44 (0)20 7554 1213
M: +44 (0)7881 783078
F: +44 (0)20 7554 1001
laura.forman@interbrand.com
www.interbrand.com

Gg
Mark Griffiths
Ideal Word
156 Evesham Road
Stratford upon Avon
Warwickshire
CV37 9BP

T: +44 (0)1789 269768
M: +44 (0)7742 528888
markgriffiths@idealword.co.uk
www.idealword.co.uk

Hh
Martin Lee
Acacia Avenue
8 Wellgarth Road
London
NW11 7HS

T: +44 (0)7940 574745
F: +44 (0)20 8731 6313
martin@acacia-avenue.com
www.acacia-avenue.com

Ii
Jim Davies
totalcontent
Studio
The Abbey
Warwick Road
Southam
Warwickshire
CV47 0HN

T: +44 (0)1926 812286
F: +44 (0)1926 811386
jim@totalcontent.co.uk
www.totalcontent.co.uk

Jj
Will Awdry
DDB London
12 Bishops Bridge Road
London
W2 6AA

T: +44 (0)207 258 4420
F: +44 (0)207 258 4447
will.awdry@ddblondon.com
www.ddblondon.com

Kk
Neil Taylor
The Writer
100 Borough High Street
London
SE1 1LB

T: +44 (0)7779 279847
F: +44 (0)20 7863 3088
neil.taylor@thewriter.co.uk
www.thewriter.co.uk

Ll
Mary Whenman
Fleishman-Hillard
40 Long Acre
London
WC2E 9LG

T: +44 (0)20 7395 7036
F: +44 (0)20 7497 0096
whenmanm@fleishman.com
www.fleishman.com

Mm
Sarah McCartney
Little Max

sarah@littlemax.co.uk
www.littlemax.co.uk

Nn
John Simmons
26 Grasmere Road
London
N10 2DJ

T: +44 (0)20 8245 0835
M: +44 (0)7976 916502
john.simmons@thewriter.co.uk
www.theinvisiblegrail.com

Oo
Tim Rich
23 Tintagel Crescent
London
SE22 8HT

T: +44 (0)7711 183636
timrich@btconnect.com

Pp
Robert Williams
Penguin
80 Strand
London
WC2R 0RL

T: +44 (0)20 7010 3437
F: +44 (0)20 7010 6708
robert.williams@penguin.co.uk
www.penguin.co.uk

Qq
Jamie Jauncey
Cairnlea
Perth Road
Birnam
Dunkeld
PH8 0BH

T: +44 (0)1350 728041
F: +44 (0)1350 728042
jamie@jauncey.co.uk
www.jauncey.co.uk

Rr
Roger Horberry
rogerhorberry@hotmail.com

Ss
Howard Fletcher
Studio 9
9a Dallington Street
London
EC1V 0BQ

T: +44 (0)20 7490 1767
F: +44 (0)20 7490 1767
hfletcher@atlas.co.uk
www.howardfletcher.co.uk

Tt
John Spencer
Spencer du Bois Limited
Gensurco House
52–54 Rosebery Avenue
London
EC1R 4RP

T: +44 (0)20 7843 0030
F: +44 (0)20 7837 0785
john@spencerdubois.co.uk
www.spencerdubois.co.uk

Uu
Dan Germain
innocent
3 The Goldhawk Estate
Brackenbury Road
London
W6 0BA

T: +44 (0)20 8600 3952
F: +44 (0)20 8600 3940
dan@innocentdrinks.co.uk
www.innocentdrinks.co.uk

Vv
Stuart Delves
Henzteeth
The Cottage
Bush House
Edinburgh Technopole
Edinburgh
EH26 0BB

T: +44 (0)131 445 5860
stuart@henzteeth.com
www.henzteeth.com

Ww
Dan Radley
Start
2 Sheraton Street
London
W1F 8BH

T: +44 (0)20 7269 0101
F: +44 (0)20 7269 0102
danr@startcreative.co.uk
www.startcreative.co.uk

Xx
Mike Reed
Freelance writer
94 Friern Road
London
SE22 0AX

T: +44 (0)7976 887231
mail@mreed.biz
www.mreed.biz

Yy
Margaret Oscar
PO Box 380
Torquay
TQ1 2ZX

T: +44 (0)7976 424036
F: +44 (0)7976 650065
me@margaretoscar.com

Zz
Alastair Creamer
Catalyst
Lever Fabergé and Unilever
Ice Cream & Frozen Food
3 St James's Road
Kingston-upon-Thames
Surrey
KT1 2BA

T: +44 (0)20 8439 6034
alastair.creamer@unilever.com

About Good News Press

At Good News Press we've been transforming graphic design into printed reality since 1964.

For us it all starts with words. We like to talk to designers and hear what they have to say. We want to understand what they're trying to achieve. Then we can think about how we might help them find more reliable, economical and interesting ways to produce their work.

Our clients know we're always delighted to give input early in the design process. We're happy to advise on anything from a short-run mailer to a major annual report, even at pitch stage.

We work in the same open way with our suppliers. For example, we're constantly researching and discussing new stocks, materials and printing methods with the best paper merchants and manufacturers.

Of course, the end result is the ultimate measure of what we do as some of our clients' testimonials show.

Then there's this book, *26 Letters*, a celebration of what happens when words and design meet. It's something we're proud to be involved in, and it's another example of what we can do. If you like what you see here and want to know more, you can contact our sales director, Dean Chappell, at:

Good News Press
Hallsford Bridge
Ongar
Essex
CM5 9RX

T: +44 (0)1277 362106
F: +44 (0)1277 354990
dean@goodnewspress.co.uk
www.goodnewspress.co.uk

"This was a demanding job that needed constant care and attention, from initial quotes through to final delivery. Good News excelled at every level. Good quality, good service and most of all good collaborators, who worked with us to produce a beautifully printed book."

Client: Sean Perkins, North Design
Project: Manhattan Loft, 10 Years Celebration brochure

"We involved Good News early in the process. They know the importance I place on print quality and they are not afraid of that. They again lived up to their reputation for attention to detail and the result is a stunning piece of work."

Client: Martin Muir, Start Creative
Project: Virgin Upper Class Suite launch brochure

"This was an important project for a prestigious client. Naturally, we wanted to make an impression and we were careful to choose the right printer. Good News has always delivered in the past and despite the size of the project and the inevitable tight schedule, they tackled the job with ease."

Client: Tim Watson, Duffy
Project: Sony Centres brand book